A GIFT FROM GOD

FOR OUR TIMES

The Life and Mission
of St. Faustina

Sister M. Elżbieta Siepak O.L.M.

A GIFT FROM GOD
FOR OUR TIMES

The Life and Mission
of St. Faustina

Wydawnictwo *Misericordia*

Kraków 2007

Title of the original
Dar Boga dla naszych czasów.
Życie i misja świętej Siostry Faustyny.

Compiled by
Sister M. Elżbieta Siepak O.L.M.

Translated by
Teresa Bałuk-Ulewiczowa

© Zgromadzenie Sióstr Matki Bożej Miłosierdzia
ul. Żytnia 3/9, 01-014 Warszawa

Cover
Andrzej Oczkoś

Nihil obstat
Rev. Jan Machniak

Imprimatur
Bishop Jan Zając

Kraków, 15 February 2007   Nr 433/2007

Wydawnictwo *Misericordia*
Zgromadzenia Sióstr Matki Bożej Miłosierdzia
ul. Siostry Faustyny 3, 30-420 Kraków
tf.: (012) 267 61 01
e-mail: misericordia@faustyna.pl
on-line bookshop: www.misericordia.faustyna.pl

Distribution
Congregation of the Sisters of Our Lady of Mercy
241 Neponset Ave., Dorchester, MA 02122, USA
www.sisterfaustina.org

ISBN 978-83-89731-41-8

Table of Contents

Introduction

Apostle of Divine Mercy, Prophet of Our Times, Great Mystic, Mistress of Spiritual Life – these are the epithets usually appended to the name of Sister Faustyna Kowalska, St. Faustyna (Faustina), of the Congregation of the Sisters of Our Lady of Mercy. Sister Faustina is one of the Church's most popular and widely known saints. She is generally associated with goodness and mercy, and an exceptionally strong power of intercession with the Divine Majesty. Her writings are read both by scholars and ordinary people for the depth of her union with God and the mystery of His Merciful Love for Man, which is portrayed in her *Diary* through her personal mystical experience. Her school of spirituality finds a following not only in those who discover in themselves the charism of spreading God's Merciful Love in the world, but also those who have lost their way and are trying to find a light in the darkness and hope for a better, more meaningful life.

Sister Faustina's principal task was to pass on to the Church and world the Message of Mercy, a recapitulation of the Biblical truth of God's Merciful Love for every human being, and a calling to each of us to entrust our lives to Him and to actively love our neighbour. Jesus not only revealed the depth of His Mercy to St. Faustina, but also gave her new forms of worship: the picture inscribed *Jesus, I trust in You*, the Feast of Divine Mercy, the Chaplet of Divine Mercy, and the Prayer in the Hour of His Death on the Cross, the Hour of Mercy. To each of these forms of worship, as well as to the preaching of the message of Mercy through the testimony of our life, works, words, and prayer, He attached great promises, on condition that we put our trust in His will and show mercy to our neighbours. In his book *Memory and Identity* the Holy Father John Paul II wrote that in the age of totalitarianisms Sister Faustina became the ambassador of the message that the only power strong enough to counteract their evil is the truth of God's Mercy. He called her *Diary* "a Gospel of Mercy written from a 20th-century perspective," which has helped people to survive the extremely painful experiences of these times. "This message," Pope Benedict XVI has said, "the message of Mercy as the Divine Power, as God putting a check on all the world's evil, is indeed the chief message precisely for our times."

This book shows St. Faustina's life and mission in a simple and straightforward way on the basis of source materials from the archives of the Congregation of the Sisters of Our Lady of Mercy. It has been written in response to the needs of the pilgrims who come to the Shrine of the Divine Mercy at Łagiewniki, Kraków, for those who wish to learn about the "Gift of God for our times," as John Paul II has called Sister Faustina.

1.

A Blessed Child

There was nothing unusual to show that the child that came into the world at Głogowiec on 25th August 1905 had been chosen by God for a special mission. Though Marianna Kowalska claimed that she considered the very easy birth, after the two previous ones in which she had nearly lost her life, to be such a sign. She had had to wait ten years for her first child. "That blessed child sanctified my womb," she said years later. All her subsequent children – another seven – were born with no further trouble.

Stanisław Kowalski married his wife at Dąbie on the River Ner. He had three brothers, lived in Kraski, and worked in a brewery at Mniewo, where he met his wife Marianna, the only child of the Babel family. After the wedding they bought a few acres of farmland in the village of Głogowiec, far away from towns and busy thoroughfares. The houses of the local smallholders lined one side of the country road, and a flat landscape of fields and meadows closed off on the horizon by a stretch of pinewood spread out on the other side. The Kowalski household, with a single-storey cottage in white brickwork and farm buildings typical for the area, soon joined the others.

The nearest church, at Świnice Warckie, was about 2 km away along a country road. All the Kowalski children were baptised in the Parish Church of St. Casimir; here they made their First Holy Communion and attended Mass on Sundays and holy days. The parish priest, Father Józef Chodyński, made the following entry for 27 August 1905 in the parish register: "On this day, 27 August 1905, at one o'clock in the afternoon, Stanisław Kowalski, farmer, aged 45 years, came accompanied by Franciszek Bednarek, aged 35 years, and Józef Stasiak, farmers of Głogowiec, presenting to us an infant of the female sex, born of his wife Marianna née Babel, aged 35, at eight o'clock in the morning of 25 August 1905 in the village of Głogowiec. The child received the name Helena in Holy Baptism administered on this day, and the godparents were Konstanty Bednarek and Marianna Szewczyk (Szczepaniak)."

Life in the Kowalski household went on at a tranquil pace marked out first by prayer and then work, never the other way round. God came first, not only on Sundays and family occasions, but every day. In the early morning Father would sing the Hours or other hymns, and when Mother rebuked him that he would wake the children, he replied that they had to learn from their youngest years that God was the most important. There were holy pictures on the walls, and a little altar stood in the middle of the bedroom, with a crucifix and two holy statues, the Sacred Heart of Jesus and the Immaculate Heart of Mary, which Father had bought in Częstochowa. At night the whole family would kneel for evening prayers, in May they would sing the Loreto Litany in front of the outdoor chapel outside the house, and in October recite the rosary. On Sunday afternoons Father would take out the Lives of the Saints from the bookcase and read aloud.

To keep his large family Father supplemented his income from the farm with work as a carpenter. He was strict with himself and his children and did not tolerate even the slightest misdemeanour. When little Stasio picked some willow branches from a neighbour's tree, he was sternly reprimanded to make him remember to treat other people's property as if it were his own. Mother ran the house and brought the children up. With her inborn gentleness, she trained them from their youngest years in jobs about the house and farm, and responsibility in carrying out their duties. Although she could not read she was the one who instructed them in the faith and the principles of morality, and prepared them for their First Holy Communion. All the parish priest had to do was to test their religious knowledge before admitting them to the Sacrament.

That was the family atmosphere of little Helenka, God's chosen one to be the prophet of our times. But there was something that set her apart from the rest of the children in the village. Her mother noticed that she loved to pray and would even get up at night and kneel down. When she tried to curb her daughter's enthusiasm saying, "You'll go mad if you keep getting up in the middle of the night," Helenka told her, "Mummy, it must be an angel that wakes me up for prayers." At the age of seven she had her first undeniable experience of God's love. "Once, when I was seven years old, at a Vesper Service, conducted before the Lord Jesus in the monstrance, the love of God was imparted to me for the first time and filled my little heart; and the Lord gave me understanding of divine things." She prepared with deep reverence for her First Holy Communion, which was administered to her by

Father Roman Pawłowski during a ceremony in the Parish Church. She returned home aware of the Divine Visitor in her soul. When a friend asked her why she was walking alone, not with the other girls, she said, "I'm not alone, I'm walking with Jesus." Her friend was happy that she had a fine new dress, but Helenka said she was happy because for the first time in her life she had received Jesus. Her awareness of the presence of God in her soul could be observed already in childhood, and grew throughout her life, just as did her responsiveness to the needs of others.

When she was still a little girl she already had a palpable "sense of mercy." She would notice the poor people and those in need around her, who came into the village for a piece of bread and a donation of any kind. Not only did she notice them, but she would also think of ways to help them. One day she held a lottery, another time she put on her mother's old clothes and went from house to house begging. She gave the money she had collected to the parish priest for the poor. She was eager to help her parents and so as not to make them unhappy would do even those chores her siblings had shirked. "Everyone loved her, "her mother recalled, "she was chosen, the best of the children. She was modest and quiet, ready to do any chore and help anyone, but at the same time cheerful and always with a smile on her face."

Not only her parents noticed little Helenka's goodness, and her open attitude to God and other people. "You have a good, humble and such an innocent child," a neighbour, Marianna Berezińska, praised Helenka. "Kowalska has such a blessed child!" she used to say in the village. Her siblings and peers also saw that Helenka was someone with a different mentality, who did not go to village dances and liked to pray and read the lives of the saints. "From her youngest years she would tell us about the saints, pilgrims, and hermits who fed only on roots, berries and forest honey," her brother Stanisław recalled. "When she wanted to please her father she would take the Lives of the Saints or some other religious book from our modest bookcase and read aloud. She memorised the stories of the hermits and missionaries, and the next day while out grazing the cattle would recite them word for word to us and others. She told us children that when she grew up she would enter a convent, but we laughed. We did not understand her."

Helenka went to school in 1917, aged twelve, when the area was liberated from Russian occupation and a primary school was established in Świnice Warckie. Her father had already taught her to read, but at school she had the opportunity to learn more. She was an able pupil and a keen learner, but had to leave after just three years to make room for the younger children. The family was not well off, so like her older sisters she went into domestic service.

2.

Extraordinary Light

At the age of sixteen Helenka bade farewell to her parents, brothers and sisters and left home for Aleksandrów Łódzki, a town where Kazimierz Bryszewski and his wife Leokadia, relatives of Marcin Ługowski, a family acquaintance from nearby Rogów, had a bakery and shop at No. 30 in the Parzęczewska (now 1 Maja 7). They were not absolute strangers, but for those times it was quite far from home. The Bryszewski couple needed help with the housework and looking after their only son Zenek, who was six. "Mummy served customers in the shop," he recalled years later, "and Helenka tidied up, helped with the cooking, and had to wash up, carry out the refuse and bring water as there was no running water. She also brought in food for employees who were provided with meals by my parents. If time allowed she would play with me.

She had a lot of work, as there were four rooms in the house, the shop, and the bakery."

She had servant's quarters in the kitchen, which had a window onto the bakery yard. One day she saw an extraordinary light there. Her commonsense told her it must be a fire and she started shouting just when the bakers were putting the loaves into the oven. They ran out, but it turned out to be a false alarm. There was no fire in the yard. But Helenka took it so badly a doctor had to be called and her parents informed. They were so worried they sent their eldest daughter Józefa to find out what had happened. But all Helenka said was that she had seen a great light. She asked her sister to tell her parents that she was not stupid but would not be staying much longer in the house.

She returned to Głogowiec to ask her parents' permission to enter a convent. Though they were god-fearing, the Kowalskis were reluctant to give up their best child. They gave an excuse of not being able to afford a dowry and refused permission. Helenka tried to persuade them that it was not a question of money, as Jesus would settle that problem, but her father was adamant. He did not even listen to the parish priest's advice to sell a cow and let the girl enter a convent, since God was calling her. Helenka did not want to enter without her parents' consent, so she went into service again, this time in Łódź. She stayed at the house of her uncle Michał Rapacki, at No. 9 in the Krośnieńska, and worked for three ladies who were Tertiaries of St. Francis. When she started the job she asked to be allowed time for daily Mass, visiting the sick and dying, and using the ministry of her mistresses' confessor.

On 2 February 1923 Helenka was sent by an employment agency to the house of Mrs. Marcjanna Sadowska, who had a shop at No. 29 in the Abramowskiego and needed a child-minder for her three children. When she saw a smartly dressed girl on her doorstep she thought the girl would be no good as a servant and reduced the wages offered. But Helenka was not discouraged and took up the job, living in with her employer. "Whenever I left the house," Mrs. Sadowska said of her maid years later, "I could rest assured. She was better at keeping the house than I was. She was kind, courteous, and hard-working. I've absolutely nothing to hold against her, she was just so good. Words cannot describe how good she was." Helenka looked after her employer's children and also after those in need, of whom there was no shortage. A sick man lived in a lumber room under the stairs in the house. Helenka cared for him, bringing food and a priest to look after his salvation.

When she was eighteen she once again asked her parents' permission to enter a convent and again was refused. "After this refusal, I turned myself over to the vain things of life, paying no attention to the call of grace, although my soul found no satisfaction in any of these things. The incessant call of grace caused me much anguish;" she wrote in her diary, "I tried, however, to stifle it with amusements. Interiorly, I shunned God, turning with all my heart to creatures." So she did not turn down an invitation to a dance in the Wenecja Park. There were three sisters from the Kowalski family in service at the time in Łódź, each in a different house: Helenka and Gienia in opposite houses on the same street, and Natalka on the Nawrot. They usually met on Sundays after Mass in the cathedral for a chat, which they had no time for during the week. Gienia, who liked dancing, knew there were dances in the Wenecja Park, which was privately owned and was an entertainment centre for the people of Łódź and its environs. In the mornings it served as a children's playground; on Sundays and holiday afternoons bands played in the open-air concert precinct, and in the evenings there would be dances and shows with stuntmen. The three sisters and a friend, Lucyna Strzelecka, another maid who later became Sister Julita, an Ursuline, went to one of these dances. "Helenka was in a pink cotton dress with frills at the side," Natalka recalled, "and her hair was arranged in a plait as thick as her arm at the back of her head. She had a good figure and was a cheerful and attractive girl. When we reached the dance, Gienia was at once asked to dance and we were left behind. Then two young men came up and one of them asked Helenka. She tried to excuse herself, saying that she was not a good dancer, but he said he would lead. When they finished the piece Helenka said she had to leave. I did not really understand what she meant and asked her if she wasn't imagining things, but she answered that she would not stay any longer and left."

Later Helenka shed light on her behaviour, which seemed strange at the time, at that extraordinary dance, to which Jesus "came" to speak to His chosen one and make His intentions plain to her, saying, "How long shall I suffer you and how long will you keep putting Me off?" She said she had a headache and quickly left the company, making her way to the nearest church, the Cathedral of St. Stanisław Kostka. There, ignoring the people who were present, she prostrated herself on the floor and spread her arms out in the shape of a cross before the Blessed Sacrament and begged the Lord to tell her what she was to do next. "Go at once to Warsaw;" came the answer, "you will enter a convent there."

Without asking her parents' consent she packed and told her sister of her decision to go to Warsaw. Uncle Michał Rapacki tried to talk her out of it, telling her how deeply she would hurt her parents, but this time Helenka stood her ground. She asked her uncle to say good-bye for her to her parents, and then set off for Warsaw with just the clothes she was in and a small bag.

As she got off the train at Warsaw's main station on a July evening in 1924 she was overwhelmed with anxiety. It was getting dark and she did not know anyone in Warsaw. She asked Our Lady for help and was advised to leave the city for a safe night's sleep. Opposite the railway station there was a suburban railway station for Włochy and Pruszków. Following the inspiration, she boarded a train and stayed the night with some people who lived in a suburb. Early in the morning she returned to Warsaw, got off at the stop near St. James' Church and went in. After several Masses an inspiration told her to go into the sacristy and ask the priest for advice how to look for a convent. She happened to find the parish priest, Father Jakub Dąbrowski, who having listened to her story sent her to his acquaintances, Aldona and Samuel Lipszyc, with a note saying that he did not know the girl but hoped she would be useful. Mr and Mrs Lipszyc lived in Ostrówek in the district of Klembów and needed a nanny for their children. In their house, in a spa resort with a climate beneficial for patients with cardiac disorders, Helenka found the refuge from which she set off in search of a convent, and once she had found it stayed for another year to save some money for a modest monastic trousseau. She looked after the house and the four small children when her employer was expecting the next arrival. "I remember her wholesome, happy smile, "Aldona Lipszyc recalled after many years. "She used to sing a lot and I always think of her in connection with the hymn she sang most often and which I learned from her, 'I am to revere Jesus hidden in the Sacrament, I am to give all for Him, and live by His love.'"

In the Lipszyc household Helenka was treated like a member of the family, they all loved and respected her for her hard work and cheerfulness. She had a way with children, in short – she had all it takes to be a good wife and mother. Mrs. Lipszyc tried to get her to marry. But Helenka felt her heart was so big that no human love would satisfy it. "It was during the octave of Corpus Christi," she recorded the most important event of her time at Ostrówek in her diary, "God filled my soul with the interior light of a deeper knowledge of Him as Supreme Goodness and Supreme Beauty. I came to know how very much God loves me. Eternal is His love for me. It was at vespers. In simple words, which flowed from the heart, I made to God a vow of perpetual chastity. From that moment I felt a greater intimacy with God, my Spouse. From that moment I set up a little cell in my heart where I always kept company with Jesus."

3.

*"To this place
I have called you"*

She commuted into Warsaw from Ostrówek looking for a convent which would take her. But she was turned down wherever she went. Finally she came to the house of the Congregation of the Sisters of Our Lady of Mercy. "She looked unremarkable, slightly delayed age-wise, rather feeble figure, a maidservant and cook by profession, no dowry, not even the most meagre of trousseaus. Unexceptional, a meagre little creature, poor, nothing special about her, not very promising." That's how Mother Małgorzata Gimbutt described the candidate on a preliminary interview to Mother General, Mother Leonarda Cielecka, who was not very keen on admitting persons with such a background into the Congregation. Mother Michaela Moraczewska, superior of the Warsaw house, who was present during the conversation, offered to speak to the candidate herself. Through the locutory door which was ajar she saw an unpretentious girl and at first, on observing her somewhat shabby appearance, had a mind to turn her away but it occurred to her that it would be more charitable first to talk to her. During the conversation she saw the candidate in a better light and wanted to admit her, so she advised the girl to ask the Master of the house whether He would accept her. Helenka knew this meant going to the chapel. While she prayed there she heard the words, "I do accept; you are in My Heart." When she returned to the reception room she repeated these words to Mother Superior, who said, "If the Lord has accepted, then I also will accept." Helenka's immediate entry was prevented by poverty, and Mother Superior advised her to continue for a time in service and save up for a small trousseau, testing the firmness of her vocation.

At last on 1 August 1925, the vigil of the Feast of Our Lady Queen of Angels, the day came when Helenka Kowalska crossed the threshold into the convent enclosure. "I felt immensely happy;" she confided in her diary, "it seemed to me I had stepped into the life of Paradise. A single prayer was bursting forth from my heart, one of praise." But already after three weeks she observed that there was little time in the convent for prayer, and wanted to "move to a stricter order." She wanted to inform Mother Superior of this and leave, but God arranged the circumstances in such a way that the meeting never ensued that day. At night, when she returned to her cell vexed and continuing to pray prostrating herself on the floor, she saw the tortured face of Jesus and asked, "Jesus, who has hurt You so much?" "It is you who will cause Me this pain if you leave this convent," Jesus replied. "It is to this place that I called you and nowhere else; and I have prepared many graces for you." She apologised to Jesus and immediately revoked her decision. Next day during confession the chaplain told her that clearly it was God's will she should stay in the Congregation. She accepted this with great joy, and henceforth felt happy and contented in the knowledge that such was the will of God.

Jesus had brought his chosen one into a Congregation which ever since 1862 had been rehabilitating fallen women and girls, as they were called in those days, that is educating persons in need of profound moral renewal and of their own free will wanting to transform their lives. The educative work was done by the sisters of the first choir, while the rest of the nuns, in the second choir, performed all the ancillary duties to maintain the Congregation and enable it to accomplish its apostolic work. Regardless of her individual duties, each of the sisters made an effort not only for her own sanctification, but also did all she could for the salvation of the souls the Lord had entrusted to the Congregation's care. Its Constitution said that by patiently devoting themselves to this aspect of their vocation, the sisters were providing a most commendable service and praising the Divine Majesty, since there was nothing God wanted so much as the salvation of souls, especially the souls of sinners, for whose sake He had assumed a human body.

Since she had no educational qualifications, Helenka Kowalska was admitted to the second choir and at first sent to work in the kitchen of the general house, then managed by Sister Sabina Tronina. "She performed all her duties conscientiously and did everything she was told," the head of the kitchen staff said. Sometimes during the day she would ask for a short break to go to the chapel, but was not always allowed to do so, since as a postulant she did not have to say as many prayers as the professed nuns.

After just a few weeks in the convent Mother Superior sent the postulant along with two other sisters to Skolimów, in the suburbs, for reasons of health, which had deteriorated due to the fairly strict fasts practised in the house and in service, and also due to the spiritual experience of a new life in the convent. At Skolimów she asked Jesus whom she should pray for. In reply she had a vision of purgatory, from which she learned that the greatest torment of the souls in this "misty place, full of fire" was longing for God. In her heart of hearts she heard the words, "My Mercy does not want this, but Justice demands it." From then on Helenka prayed all the more fervently for the souls in purgatory, to help them, and God permitted her to establish a closer form of contact with them.

Mother Janina Olga Bartkiewicz, a person of great wisdom and a big heart, was postulant mistress at the time, in charge of the first stage of the community's life. She was very demanding of herself and others and cloaked her goodness and magnanimity in the service of God under a mantle of sternness and severity. She was very kind to young postulants preparing for the religious life, but at the same time made big demands of them and directed them firmly. Of Helenka she used to say that she had an inner life of her very own and that her little soul must be dear to Jesus. In Community Helenka used to come into contact with other sisters and life also brought naturally unpleasant episodes. "Once, when I was in the kitchen with Sister N.," she recorded in her diary remembering her postulancy, "she got a little upset with me and, as a punishment, ordered me to sit on the table while she herself continued to work hard, cleaning and scrubbing. And while I was sitting there, the sisters came along and were astounded to find me sitting on the table, and each one had her say. One said that I was a loafer and another, 'What an eccentric!' I was a postulant at the time. Others said, 'What kind of a sister will she make?' Still, I could not get down because sister had ordered me to sit there by virtue of obedience until she told me to get down. Truly, God only knows how many acts of self-denial it took. I thought I'd die of shame. God often allowed such things for the sake of my inner formation." Sister Szymona Nalewajk, who along with Sister Marcjanna Oświęcimek had witnessed that incident in the kitchen and many more, since she and Helenka were postulants in the same period, admired Helenka for taking all the humiliations so meekly and without grumbling. "I was amazed a junior postulant was capable of such self-restraint and goodness, "she later wrote. This conduct was inspired by Helenka's fervent faith and concern to be like Jesus, Who trusted in the Heavenly Father even when He was on the cross and Who was meek and humble throughout His life, loving all people with a pa-

tient, understanding, and indescribably self-sacrificing love.

Helenka spent the last months of her postulancy in the novice house in Kraków, where she arrived on 23 January 1926. That night she was visited by a religious sister who had died, and asked
for Helenka's confessor, Father Stanisław Rospond,
to say Mass and three exclamatory prayers for her
soul. Neither exalted nor credulous, before Helenka
informed the novice mistress of this she took time
to consider whether it had not been a deception.
When the vision recurred a second and third time
she fulfilled the request, and in return, when the sister appeared yet again, she thanked Helenka.

The novice mistress at the time was Mother
Małgorzata Gimbutt, a prayerful person and de-
vout practitioner of the mortifications, meek and
quiet, who educated the young nuns entrusted to
her care above all by the example of her life. She was
the tutor who prepared Helenka to take the veil and
directed her in the first months of her novitiate.

4.

"From today on you shall be called Sister Maria Faustyna"

"From today on you shall not be called by your baptismal name, you shall be called Sister Maria Faustyna." These were the words the chaplain conducting the ceremony for the taking of the veil, on 30 April 1926, addressed to the postulant Helena Kowalska. That was the name given her by Mother General Leonarda Cielecka. Every sister received the name Maria in honour of Our Lady, but in everyday matters in and outside the Congregation the sisters used their second name, which came to be identified with them. From that day on no-one addressed Helenka by the name she had been given at baptism, but by her name in religion. "From today on you shall be called Sister Faustina." During the ceremony Helenka fainted twice. Sister Klemensa Buczek, who helped her take off her white dress and veil and put on the habit, thought it must have been due to the emotions associated with abandoning the world whereas, it turned out, it was the effect of a mystical experience. As she took the veil God let her know how much she would suffer. She saw clearly what she was taking upon herself. The suffering lasted a minute and then God again filled her soul with great comfort.

As a novice Faustina helped in the girls' kitchen. In the House of Mercy at Łagiewniki (Kraków) the sisters had well over a hundred charges, so there was plenty of work in the kitchen. Meals were cooked in huge pots and Sister Faustina could not cope with them, especially when it came to draining the potatoes. She reported this to her novice mistress, who said that she would get used to it and improve with time. But despite her efforts, as she tipped the pot some of the potatoes would tumble out, and whenever potatoes had to be drained Sister Faustina would move away and try to get out of doing this chore. One day in her prayers she complained to Jesus that she was not strong enough to perform this chore, and was told, "From today on you will do this easily; I shall strengthen you." Trustfully that same evening, when the time came to drain the potatoes, she grabbed the pot and had no problems with draining them, and when she lifted the lid to let the steam come out she saw that instead of potatoes, the pot was full of red roses. As she wondered what this could mean she heard a voice in her heart, "I change such hard work of yours into bouquets of most beautiful flowers, and their perfume rises up to My throne." From that moment on she tried to do this chore for other sisters and eagerly helped out with every other hard chore, as she had learned how pleasing this was to God.

After less than two months of Sister Faustina's novitiate there was a change of novice mistress (20 June 1926). Mother Małgorzata Gimbutt was replaced by Mother Józefa Brzoza, who had been trained for the office in Laval (France), which served the Foundress, Mother Teresa Ewa Countess Potocka née Sułkowska, as the spiritual model for the Congregation's religious life and apostolic work in Poland. The Novice Mistress' thorough training and personal experience gave her the confidence to lead the novices into the spiritual life, teaching them to know God more profoundly, to pray and practise the ascetic life, so that their piety should not be emotional and "soft" but thorough, and bring them to an ever deeper union with God through obedience, humility, a self-sacrificing love of their neighbours and a zeal for the salvation of the souls entrusted to the Congregation's apostolic care. Sister

Faustina followed the novice mistress' instructions attentively and fulfilled all the duties allotted her with exactitude. "We were together in the novitiate for a year," recalled Sister Krescencja Bogdanik, who was a year ahead of her in her vocation. "I saw how enthusiastically Sister Faustina carried out all her duties. As I was a senior novice I had to act as her guide ("angel"). I was to bring her into the life of the community, and admired her for her quick learning. You didn't have to tell her twice, as often happens with other novices. And you could always observe a childlike joy on her face." "At this time Sister Faustina often spoke of God's mercy, "Sister Szymona Nalewajk recollects, "while I would challenge her and stress His justice. But her arguments always won." Her fellow nuns called her "the lawyer" because she could direct the discussion to the subject of God's truths. They liked her and gathered around her during recreation, as her thoughts and words were focused on God and she was always cheerful.

That joy faded somewhat towards the end of her first year in the novitiate when she started to go through a period of extremely painful spiritual experiences known as the passive nights. "Toward the end of the first year of my novitiate," she recorded in her diary, "darkness began to cast its shadow over my soul. I felt no consolation in prayer; I had to make a great effort to meditate; fear began to sweep over me. Going deeper into myself, I could find nothing but great misery. I could also clearly see the great holiness of God. I did not dare to raise my eyes to Him, but cast myself into the dust under His feet and begged for mercy. ...I did not understand what I was reading; I could not meditate; it seemed to me that my prayer was displeasing to God. It seemed to me that by receiving the Holy Sacraments I was offending God even more. But despite this, my confessor did not let me omit one single Holy Communion. God was working very strangely in my soul. I did not understand anything at all of what my confessor was telling me. The simple truths of the faith became incomprehensible to me. My soul was in anguish, unable to find comfort anywhere. At a certain point, there came to me the very powerful impression that I am rejected by God. This terrible thought pierced my soul right through; in the midst of the suffering my soul began to experience the agony of death. I wanted to die but could not."

Sister Faustina was helped through these extremely painful experiences not only by her confessor, but also by her novice mistress, who correctly diagnosed her spiritual condition (which was not easy) and applied the right remedy. She instructed Sister Faustina to say the exclamatory prayers instead of long prayers which required a considerable amount of concentration, and thereby accept the will of God. She told her that God was still her Father although He was testing her, and that these trials were to prepare her soul for a fuller union with Him. And when a time of deadly tribulation and Satan's temptations came, when it seemed to Sister Faustina that she was doomed to hell, the novice mistress dragged her out of this state thanks to holy obedience and allowed her to persevere throughout that time of severe tribulation. "I trust in Your words," she confided to Jesus in the Blessed Sacrament, "because You are Truth and Life. In spite of everything, Jesus, I trust in You in the face of every interior sentiment which sets itself against hope. Do what You want with me; I will never leave You, because You are the source of my life." These experiences were a great school of faith, hope, and charity for Sister Faustina, a school of childlike trust in God. All she had to rely on was the truth that God is Love and always loves His children. Although she could not feel this, although from the human point of view everything seemed to belie this truth, although she even felt that God had rejected her, she never stopped trusting in His goodness and mercy and showed Him her trust. "Even if You kill me, still will I trust in You," she said after the biblical Job.

In these dark nights of the soul there were moments of light and joy, when God allowed her to feel His love or when Our Lady came to her aid. One such moment was the ceremony for her first vows, which was celebrated on 30 April 1928 by Bishop Stanisław Rospond. Sister Faustina's parents came to the Łagiewniki convent. It was the first time she saw them since her departure for service in Łódź. They found her full of joy and happiness. "See, Father," she said to her father, who had been so staunchly against her entry into the convent. "The One to whom I have made my vows is my husband and therefore your son-in-law." This argument and their child's happiness persuaded her parents and from then on they had no further objections to her life in the convent.

After taking her first vows Sister Faustina stayed for a few months in Kraków. In October 1928 the Congregation held its General Chapter, and the office of Mother General was entrusted to Mother Michaela Olga Moraczewska, who when she was superior of the Warsaw house had admitted Helenka Kowalska to the Congregation and been her superior during the first months of postulancy. From that year until Sister Faustina's death Mother Michaela was her superior, and not only made the decisions concerning Sister Faustina's work and place of residence, but also took part in the mission God had entrusted to her. Mother Michaela was one of the great figures in the Congregation's history. She was educated (a graduate of a music conservatory) and spoke several languages. She was magnanimous and devoted her entire life to the saving of souls. For 18 years she directed the spiritual and apostolic life of the entire Congregation which, following Sister Faustina's visions, she entrusted to the care of Mary, Mother of Mercy, the Congregation's heavenly Superior General. Sister Faustina put an immense amount of confidence in Mother Michaela, who helped her tremendously in the accomplishment of her vocation and was the woman of providence for the recognition of the mission of prophecy.

Straight after the Chapter meeting, in October 1928, Mother Michaela assigned Sister Faustina for work in the girls' kitchen of the mother house in Warsaw. The girls who worked with her there held her in great respect, as she loved them dearly and did her best to direct them to God, encourage them to make use of His goodness, and live in a state of grace. In her own spiritual life there were more and more inner voices and visions, which she tried to avoid, since she did not have a regular confessor who could help her assess these things. They included suggestions of prayers for Poland and a city under threat. "One day," she recorded in her diary, "Jesus told me that He would cause a chastisement to fall upon the most beautiful city in our country. This chastisement would be that with which God had punished Sodom and Gomorrah. I saw the great wrath of God and a shudder pierced my heart. I prayed in silence. After a moment, Jesus said to me, 'My child, unite yourself closely to Me during the Sacrifice and offer My Blood and My Wounds to My Father in expiation for the sins of that city. Repeat this without interruption throughout the entire Holy Mass. Do this for seven days.' On the seventh day I saw Jesus in a bright cloud and began to beg Him to look upon the city and upon our whole country. Jesus looked down graciously. When I saw the favourable attitude of Jesus, I began to beg His blessing. Immediately Jesus said, 'For your sake I bless the entire county.' And He made a big sign of the cross over our country. Seeing the goodness of God, a great joy filled my soul."

In the first years of her juniorate, that is after making her first religious profession, Sister Faustina worked in many of the Congregation's houses.

Early in 1929 she went to Wilno (then on Polish territory; now Vilnius, Lithuania) to replace Sister Petronela Basiura, who was leaving for her third probation; then she returned to Warsaw and the house in the Żytnia, only to be sent off to a new house on the Hetmańska in the Grochów district. In the same year she went to Kiekrz near Poznań, to take over in the kitchen for Sister Modesta Rzecz-kowska, who was ill. In December of the same year she came back to the house in the Żytnia, but not for long. "Things turned out in such a way," Mother General Michaela Moraczewska explained Sister Faustina's frequent moves, "that she had to be trans-ferred fairly often to new places, so that she worked in almost all of the Congregation's houses. After a brief stay in Warsaw in the Żytnia and at Gro-chów, she was again sent off to Płock, and from there for a short time to Biała, an agricultural colo-ny of the Płock house. Her main occupation at Płock, until her third probation, was serving cus-tomers in the baker's shop."

5.

"Paint a picture"

It was in the convent at Płock, where Sister Faustina arrived in the May or June of 1930, that her great prophetic mission was to begin. It was Sunday, 22 February 1931. In the evening when she returned to her cell, she had a physical vision of Jesus in a white robe. His right hand was lifted up in a gesture of blessing, and His left hand was touching His breast from which two rays, a red one and a pale one, radiated out. After a while Jesus said to her, "Paint an image according to the pattern you see, with the signature: 'Jesus, I trust in You.' I desire that this image be venerated, first in your chapel, and then throughout the world. I promise that the soul that venerates this image will not perish. I also promise victory over its enemies already here on earth, especially at the hour of death. I shall protect it as My own glory."

During her next confession she told her confessor about this incident. The priest told her to paint an image of Jesus in her soul. But as she left the confessional Jesus explained, "My image already is in your soul. I desire that there be a Feast of Mercy. I want this image, which you will paint with a brush, to be solemnly blessed on the first Sunday after Easter; that Sunday is to be the Feast of Mercy. I desire that priests proclaim this great mercy of Mine towards souls of sinners. Let the sinner not be afraid to approach Me. The flames of Mercy are burning me...; I want to pour them out upon souls." On Jesus' confirmation that He meant a material picture, she informed the local superior, Sister Róża Kłobukowska, about the situation, who demanded a sign confirming the truth of the visions. Jesus said to Sister Faustina that the sign would come with the graces dispensed through the picture. Sister Faustina was not good at drawing, so she asked Sister Bożenna Pniewska for help. "I couldn't paint, either, and I did not understand that she meant a new kind of picture," Sister Bożenna recalled, "so I suggested I would offer her a choice out of the many fine holy pictures I had. She thanked me but did not take up my offer."

Word went round in the Płock convent that Sister Faustina had had a vision. The other nuns in the community became sceptical with respect to her. Some warned her of hallucinations, others declared she was hysterical and fantasising, and yet others acknowledged that she must be close to Jesus since she was bearing all this suffering with such calm. "Yet, I resolved to bear everything in silence and to give no explanations when I was questioned," Sister Faustina confided in her diary, "Some were irritated by my silence, especially those who were more curious. Others, who reflected more deeply, said, 'Sister Faustina must be very close to God if she has the strength to bear so much suffering.' It was as if I were facing two groups of judges. I strove after interior and exterior silence. I said nothing about myself, even though I was questioned directly by some sisters. My lips were sealed. I suffered like a dove, without complaint."

But the greatest suffering was caused by the uncertainty as to where the visions came from. Her superiors directed her to priests, and the priests sent her back to her superiors. Sister Faustina wished a priest would come and resolve the question definitively and just say, "'Be at peace, you are on the right road,' or 'Reject all this for it does not come from God.'" In this situation, she tried to avoid the Lord, and when He came she would ask, "'Jesus, are You my God or some kind of phantom? Because my Superiors say that there are all sorts of illusions and phantoms. If You are my Lord, I beg You to bless me.' Then Jesus made a big sign of the cross over me and I, too, signed myself. When I asked pardon of Jesus for this question, He replied that I had in no way displeased Him by this question and that my confidence pleased Him very much."

The lack of a permanent spiritual director and the inability to fulfil the tasks ascribed her made Sister Faustina want to back out of these supernatural inspirations, but Jesus patiently kept on explaining to her the magnitude of the work He had chosen her for. "Know that if you neglect the matter of the painting of the image and the whole work of mercy, you will have to answer for a multitude of souls on the day of judgement," He told her. These words filled her soul with a terrible awe. She realised that she was responsible not only for her own salvation, but also other people's, and so she resolved to do all in her power to fulfil His will or to make Him transfer these graces to someone else, since she was only wasting them.

In November 1932 Sister Faustina left Płock and returned to Warsaw for the "third probation" and to prepare for her perpetual vows. Since she had not yet made her retreat that year, her superiors sent her first to the Congregation's house in nearby Walendów, where an eight-day annual retreat was just starting under the direction of the Jesuit Father Edmund Elter, a professor of ethics, homiletics and rhetoric at the Gregorianum University in Rome. Instructed in advance by Jesus, she knew that on the second day of this retreat she was to go to confession and tell this priest all about the misgivings she was having in connection with the visions, and that through his lips she would receive confirmation of the supernatural origins of the mission required of her. She fought a spiritual battle with herself before this groundbreaking confession.

"Satan is trying to persuade me," she wrote in her diary, "into believing that if my superiors have told me that my inner life is an illusion, why should I ask again and trouble the confessor? Didn't Mother X. tell you that the Lord Jesus does not commune with souls as miserable as yours? This confessor is going to tell you the same thing. Why speak to him about all this? These are not sins, and Mother X. told you that all this communing with the Lord Jesus was daydreaming and pure hysteria. So why tell it to this confessor? You would do better to dismiss all this as illusions. Look how many humiliations you have suffered because of them, and how many more are still awaiting you, and all the sisters know that you are a hysteric."

Vexed by such nagging thoughts, she begged Jesus' help, and when the conference finished and the priest took his place in the confessional she immediately rose from her kneeler and started her confession. Father Elter assured her she was on the right road, and that her relationship with Jesus was neither hysteria, nor delusion, nor daydreaming. He advised her to be true to these graces, urging her not to stay away from them but to entreat God for a spiritual director who would help her in understanding and carrying out Jesus' wishes. After this confession great joy filled her soul, at last she had obtained what she had longed for: a priest had authoritatively declared on behalf of the Church that her visions came from God and that it was God who was entrusting her with a great mission. Her joy was augmented by the mystical sense of having the Three Persons of the Holy Trinity in her soul, and such profound peace that she wondered how she could have been so worried before.

After the retreat she returned to Warsaw full of gratitude and spiritual joy to prepare during her third probation, along with two other sisters, under the direction of Mother Małgorzata Gimbutt, for the making of her perpetual vows. This five-month period was full of prayer, intensive self-improvement, conferences with the novice mistress, and other work which did not make any spiritual demands of her. She worked in the convent's vestiary, helping Sister Zuzanna Tokarska. As she repaired clothes she enriched herself spiritually through acts of mortification and penance, and as she rendered services for older or sick sisters, she occasionally witnessed human moral frailty. One of these episodes is described in her diary: "Today I was cleaning the room of one of the sisters. Although I was trying to clean it with utmost care, she kept following me all the time and saying, 'You've left a speck of dust here and a spot on the floor there.' At each of her remarks I did each place over a dozen times just to satisfy her. It is not work that makes me tired, but all this talking and excessive demands. My whole day's martyrdom was not enough for her, she went to the Directress and complained, 'Mother, who is this careless sister who doesn't know how to work quickly?' The next day, I went again to do the same job, without trying to explain myself. When she started driving me, I thought, 'Jesus, one can be a silent martyr; it is not the work that wears you out, but this kind of martyrdom.'"

Nonetheless, she took all her experiences in a spirit of faith, and offered up all the suffering and hardships as a posy for Jesus for the day of her vows. Nothing was too hard for her as a proof of her love for her Bridegroom.

Towards the end of April 1933 she came to Kraków for an eight-day retreat which was to be followed by her perpetual vows. Her heart was filled with great joy and gratitude for the grace of a vocation. God had allowed her to know the vastness of His love, which is eternal, great, pure, and disinterested, whereas her own love had grown with time as she came to know Him better.

"Each time I call to mind," she confessed, "that in a few days I am to become one with the Lord through perpetual vows, a joy beyond all description floods my soul."

The ceremony for her perpetual vows, the most important event for every sister and a festive day for the whole community, was conducted by Bishop Stanisław Rospond on 1 May 1933. Lying prostrate on the chapel floor under a black pall and with the bells tolling for the dead, the sisters about to make their final vows were dying to the world, henceforth to live only for God and His Kingdom in human hearts on earth. Each of them made her own entreaties, in the belief that at such a moment there was nothing Jesus would deny His brides. Sister Faustina commended the whole Church, her Congregation, her family, all sinners, the dying and the souls in purgatory. She thanked Jesus for the unfathomed grace of being the bride of the Son of

God and for the royal insignia – the sword, the cross, and the crown of thorns – which from henceforth would be her decoration. She implored Our Lady for special care, reminding her of a new claim to her love. "Mother of God, Most Holy Mother, You are my Mother in a special way now because Your beloved Son is my Bridegroom, and thus we are both Your children. For Your Son's sake, You have to love me. O Mary, my dearest Mother, guide my spiritual life in such a way that it will please Your Son." The Bishop bestowed on her the candle, sign of heavenly enlightenment and the flame of love, and a ring with the name "Jesus" engraved on it. "I espouse thee to Jesus Christ, Son of the Almighty Father," said Bishop Rospond as he gave her the ring. From that moment her union with God was closer than ever before. She felt that she loved God and was loved in return. Having tasted of God, her soul would not have been able to live without Him.

6.

Fulfilled requests

After her perpetual vows Sister Faustina stayed in Kraków for almost a month. Before her departure for Vilnius on 27 May 1933 she sought the advice of her confessor, Father Józef Andrasz SJ, who like Father Edmund Elter had confirmed her in the belief that the visions were genuine and advised her to remain faithful to the grace of God and be obedient. She was sorry to leave the Kraków house, where she had received so many graces and felt secure under the guidance of an experienced confessor, but Jesus assured her of His presence and promised her a priest who would help her fulfil God's will.

On her way to Vilnius she made a stop at Częstochowa. For the first time in her life she could see the Holy Image of the Virgin and Child, listen to Mary's message to her and confide in her. "The

Mother of God told me many things," she wrote in her diary. "I entrusted my perpetual vows to Her. I felt that I was Her child and that She was my Mother." Time passed relentlessly. Lost in contemplation, Sister Faustina did not notice that she had spent six hours in the shrine at Jasna Góra. Her superior was worried and sent out another sister to collect her so that she could have breakfast and catch her train.

It was her second time in the Congregation's Vilnian house in Antokol. Compared with the edifices of the Cracovian convent, the ones here gave the impression of a "cluster of tiny cottages." The lowliest was a wooden dacha with three dormitories for the sisters and the chaplain's quarters through a separate entrance across the corridor. This time Sister Faustina was to work in the garden, although she had never done any gardening before and knew nothing about it. She accepted God's will in a spirit of faith, trusting that Jesus would help and bring her in touch with people who would tell her when and what to do to make beautiful flowers and wholesome fruit and vegetables grow in the garden.

But this wasn't her biggest worry. She was anxious to fulfil the mission Jesus had given her. She waited for the priest He had promised and the chance to have the painting of the Merciful Jesus made according to God's will. "The week for confession came," she recorded in her diary, "and, to my great joy, I saw the priest I had known before coming to Vilnius. I had known him by seeing him in a vision. At that moment, I heard these words in my soul: 'This is My faithful servant, He will help you to fulfil My will here on earth.' Yet, I did not open myself to him as the Lord wished. And for some time I struggled against grace."

It was Father Michał Sopoćko, who lectured in pastoral theology in the Faculty of Theology of the Stefan Batory University, and in educational studies in a teachers' training college. He was spiritual director and chaplain in the Vilnian archdiocesan seminary, and confessor to numerous religious congregations, including the Antokol house of the Congregation of the Sisters of Our Lady of Mercy for their confession week. On his first encounters with Sister Faustina he, too, went through a period of spiritual struggle and wanted to withdraw from hearing the confessions of such an extraordinary penitent. "Right at the start she told me," he recalled, "that she had known me for a long time from a vision, that I was to be her spiritual director and accomplish some of God's plans which she would make known. I turned a deaf ear to her story and put her to a test the result of which was that on her superior's consent Sister Faustina started to look for a new confessor. After some time she returned to me and said that she would put up with anything but would not give up my ministry."

An experienced confessor and spiritual director, Father Sopoćko first tried to get to know his penitent, and not be misled by any delusions, hallucinations or fantasies deriving from human nature. He consulted Mother Superior Irena Krzyżanowska, asking for information concerning Sister Faustina's religious life and asked for an examination to be done of her physical and mental health. When all the opinions, including a psychiatric examination carried out by Dr. Helena Maciejewska, turned out in Sister Faustina's favour, Father Sopoćko still deferred for some time. He couldn't quite believe it all and make up his mind; he prayed and while keeping the particulars of the visions and penitent fully confidential sought the advice of knowledgeable priests. Finally, as he later disclosed, "More out of curiosity rather than conviction as to the authenticity of Sister Faustina's visions, I decided to have the picture painted. I got in touch with Eugeniusz Kazimirowski, an artist who lived in the same house as I and undertook to paint the picture, and with Mother Superior, who allowed Sister

Faustina to visit him twice a week to instruct him on the details of the painting."

The painting of the first picture of the Merciful Jesus started very discreetly at the beginning of January 1934. Mother Superior Irena Krzyżanowska wrote, "So as not to attract other sisters' attention to Sister Faustina's inner experiences, every Saturday morning I would go with her to Holy Mass at Ostra Brama, and afterwards we would visit the artist, who was given detailed instructions by Sister Faustina how to paint the picture of the Merciful Jesus. He did his best to follow all her requirements."

The painting of the vision Sister Faustina had had three years earlier at Płock gave rise to several fundamental questions which Father Sopoćko put to Sister Faustina, and she in the simplicity of her heart passed them on to Jesus, who explained, "My gaze from this image is like my gaze from the cross." "The two rays denote Blood and Water. The pale ray stands for the Water which justifies souls; The red ray stands for the Blood which is the life of souls..." But there were still some doubts as to the inscription. Father Sopoćko requested Sister Faustina to ask Jesus about that, too. She wrote in her diary, "Jesus reminded me of what He had told me the first time; namely, that these ...words must be clearly in evidence: 'Jesus, I trust in You.'"

After a few months, in June 1934, the work on the painting was drawing to a close. But Sister Faustina was not pleased, although the artist and Father Sopoćko did all they could to render as faithful an image of Jesus as possible. When she returned to the convent chapel, she complained to Jesus, "Who will paint You as beautiful as You are?" and was told. "Not in the beauty of the colour, nor of the brush lies the greatness of this image, but in My grace."

When the painting was completed Father Sopoćko put it up in a dark corridor in the Observantine Convent next to St. Michael's Church, of which he was rector. "It was a picture with a new content," he recalled, "and that is why I could not display it in a church without permission from the Archbishop, whom I was embarrassed to ask or, even more, to explain its origins." But Sister Faustina, urged on by Jesus, demanded it be put up in church. In the Holy Week of 1935 she told Father Sopoćko that this was what Jesus wanted and insisted it be set up for three days in the Ostra Brama gate, where a triduum of ceremonies was to be held before the first Sunday after Easter to mark the close of the Jubilee of the World's Redemption. "Soon afterwards I heard that this triduum was indeed to be celebrated," Father Sopoćko wrote, "and Canon Stanisław Zawadzki, parish priest of Ostra Brama, invited me to deliver a sermon. I agreed on condition that the painting be put up to decorate the window of the arcade. It looked impressive there, and attracted people's attention more than the image of Our Lady over the gate."

On the day before the picture was displayed Sister Faustina and one of the pupils prepared some fresh green branches and went to Ostra Brama to help decorate it. Next day some laywomen asked sisters from the Congregation about the fine picture and what it meant, as they were sure to know since one of them had decorated the picture. They suspected it must have been Sister Faustina, who would know all about it. But she remained silent, since she could not tell them the truth. "My silence," she recorded, "increased their curiosity, and I was even more on my guard not to tell a lie and not to tell the truth, since I had no permission to do so. Then they started to show their displeasure and reproached me openly saying, 'How is it that outsiders know about this and we, nothing?' Various judgements were being made about me. I suffered much for three days, but a special strength entered my soul. I am happy to suffer for God and for the souls that have been granted His mercy during these days."

But the joy of those days for Sister Faustina was the fact that Jesus' requests had been fulfilled. The

Mercy picture had been put up for public worship in the most important place in the whole of Vilnius, the Shrine of Our Lady of Ostra Brama. Father Sopoćko had preached a sermon on the Divine Mercy, during which Sister Faustina saw Jesus in the painting assume a living form, and His rays penetrate into the hearts of the people gathered for the ceremony, making them happy. He said to her, "You are a witness of My mercy. You shall stand before My throne forever as a living witness to My mercy." The powers of hell responded to the event as well. On her way home a crowd of devils stood in her way and threatened to bring down terrible torments on her. She had erased all the work they had done for years. When asked where they all came from in such numbers, they said it was from human hearts. She called her Guardian Angel, who assured her that the devil could do nothing without the will of God and visibly escorted her home. In the evening in a prophetic vision she saw the painting move over the city, which was "covered with what appeared to be a mesh and nets. As Jesus passed He cut through all the nets and finally made a large sign of the cross and disappeared."

7.

Everyday life

Big celebrations were a rarity in Sister Faustina's life. It was full of humdrum, everyday things
marked out by the old rhythm of the religious rule
which ascribed the time for prayer, work, and recreation. The day started early: up at 5 a.m. followed
by community prayers in the chapel, contemplation and Holy Mass, and then breakfast and work
until the midday examination of conscience. After
lunch there was a short spell of recreation, prayers,
and work until supper. Every evening there was Bene-
diction, followed by time for individual prayer and
a short period of evening recreation. All day long,
except for the recreation times, the rule was con-
ventual silence, which meant that the sisters could
communicate quietly. From 9 p.m. to the end of
morning Mass they were obliged to observe canon-
ical (absolute) silence. Sister Faustina adhered to

the Congregation's rules very strictly, especially the silence rule which allowed her to hear God's voice in her soul and unite with Him more closely. "In order to hear the voice of God, one has to have silence in one's soul and to keep silence; not a gloomy silence, but an interior silence, that is to say, recollection in God. One can speak a great deal without breaking silence, and, on the contrary, one can speak little and be constantly breaking silence. Oh, what irreparable damage is done by the breach of silence! We cause a lot of harm to our neighbour, but even more to ourselves."

The mantle of ordinary, everyday things cloaked an extremely rich, spectacular spiritual life aspiring to the heights of mysticism. Instructed by Jesus, Sister Faustina soon learned that the essence of human life on earth was union with God, and the individual's greatness did not depend on externals such as social status, education, office, or even great achievements, but on the degree to which he was united with God in love. Union with God was her life's fundamental aim, and she was able to put it before all the other matters and everyday events.

The foundation of her everyday life was faith, which she was continually enhancing, the fruit of which was love of God and her neighbours. Ever since childhood she had been overwhelmed by a great desire to know God, which she satisfied by a variety of very simple methods, such as the contemplation of the word of God, the mysteries of the Rosary and the Stations of the Cross, reading religious books and reflection on her own life. Living through everyday events in a spirit of active faith permitted her to see the loving hand of God in everything. "O God, how generously Your mercy is spread everywhere," she confessed in her prayers, "and You have done all this for Man. Oh, how much You must love him, since Your love is so active on his behalf. O my Creator and Lord, I see on all sides the trace of Your hand and the seal of Your mercy, which embraces all created things." She was always being astonished to discover God's merciful love in the incarnation and birth of the Son of God, in His passion, death, and resurrection, in the abundance of graces deposited in the Church, and in Man's vocation to live in union with Him on earth and for all eternity. God allowed her to witness His justice, holiness, and mercy. "And I understood," she wrote in her diary, "that the greatest attribute is love and mercy. It unites the creature with the Creator. This immense love and depth of mercy are made known to me in the Incarnation of the Word and in the Redemption and it is here that I saw this as the greatest of all God's attributes."

Learning God through the mystery of His mercy led her to the discovery of the truth that He lives in the souls of the just, as St. John wrote in his gospel. Jesus Himself confirmed her in the awareness of this unfathomable reality: "My daughter, know without doubt, and once and for all, that only mortal sin drives Me out of a soul, and nothing else." Sister Faustina was also taught by Our Lady how to practise this kind of union with God in her soul. The truth that God's merciful love for Man is so great that He stoops to inhabit the human soul led her to the contemplation of God in the ordinary things of life. "I look for no happiness," she wrote, "beyond my own interior where God dwells. I rejoice that God dwells within me; here I abide with Him unendingly; it is here that my greatest intimacy with Him exists; here I dwell with him in safety; here is a place not probed by the human eye. The Blessed Virgin encourages me to commune with God in this way." Being with God in her soul helped her to live her whole life with Jesus. The One whom she loved and to whom she had been espoused was closer than any human. For Sister Faustina he was the source of all happiness, joy and peace, light and strength in the hardships of everyday life, in times of darkness and suffering.

In the contemplation of God in her everyday business she practised a very simple rule: every month she would choose a different exclamatory prayer, e.g. "Jesus, I trust in You; Jesus, enkindle my heart with love." and apply it to unite in full awareness and love with Jesus living in her soul. "This practice gives me unusual strength; my heart is always united with the One it desires, and its actions are regulated by mercy, which flows from love," she confided. When she tried to abandon this practice Jesus told her not to. He also instructed her to combine her own prayers, fasts, mortifications, work, and all that she suffered with His prayers, fasts, mortifications, work, and suffering, so that everything in her life should be empowered before the Heavenly Father. In the life of Sister Faustina this extremely simple and ancient practice, known as standing in the presence of God or continual prayer, took on the hue of mercy, reflected not only in her personal dwelling with God in her own soul, but also being with Him when He was hidden in the souls of other people and in events. In her life it was a perpetual, beautiful dialogue of mercy, always initiated by Jesus and faithfully responded to by Sister Faustina.

Her great longing to discover God and the efforts she made to achieve this were strengthened by a bequest of contemplation, thanks to which Sister Faustina was able to enter very deeply into the mystery of Divine Mercy and then let the world learn of it. "Penetrate My mysteries, and you will know the profundity of My mercy towards creatures and My unfathomable goodness – and this you shall make known to the world," said Jesus and through contemplation let her discover His love for Man. On her confessors' advice and with the consent of her superiors she kept a diary in which she made records not only of particular meetings with the supernatural world – Jesus, Mary, the angels, saints, and souls in purgatory – but also of the prophetic mission of Mercy Jesus entrusted her with, as well as her personal prayers and reflections on the love of God and Mankind. One day, as she was making an entry in the diary, she saw Jesus bending over her. He asked, "My daughter, what are you writing?" She replied, "I am writing about You, Jesus, about Your being hidden in the Blessed Sacrament, about Your inconceivable love and mercy for people." He said, "Secretary of My most profound mystery, know that yours is an exclusive intimacy with Me. Your task is to write down everything that I make known to you about My mercy, for the benefit of those who by reading these things will be comforted in their souls and will have the courage to approach Me. I therefore want you to devote all your free moments to writing." For four years Sister Faustina conscientiously noted down the words of Jesus and her own spiritual experiences, filling up seven copy-books which make up a rich source for the discovery of God in the mystery of His Mercy.

Getting to know God, the Father rich in mercy, gave rise to and developed Sister Faustina's attitude of childlike trust in Him. "God is my Father," she wrote, "and so I, His child, have every claim to His divine Heart; and the greater the darkness, the more complete our trust should be." Although as the years passed her understanding of her own weakness and misery grew she did not become discouraged for she lived in the truth; she knew that all that was good in and around her came from God and was a grace from Him, that is why she kept one eye on the depth of her own misery, and the other on the profundity of Divine Mercy which is capable of leading Man out from his most wretched misery to the heights of sanctity. She endeavoured to trust in God always, not only in the good times but above all in times of suffering. Whenever spiritual darkness engulfed her and when the burden of her cross weighed down on her, she did not turn to people for consolation. She put all her trust in God, and so, especially in times of tribulation, she would repeat, "Jesus is good and full of mercy, and even if the ground were to give way under my feet, I would not cease to trust in Him." Her trust in God grew out of the living faith that enabled her to know Him as a loving Father, from a hope which assured her of His assistance on the road to union with Him, a love which was her response to God's eternal and ever faithful love, a humility which allowed her to face the truth, and a contrition which did not seek to justify her failings but immersed her human insignificance and misery in the depths of the Redeemer's mercy. Childlike and unconditional trust was the characteristic of her entire communion with God, and it was expressed not through the emotions, not only in prayerful exaltation and declarations, but above all in the concrete fulfilment of God's will which, as she often said, is "Mercy itself." With so many graces bestowed upon her, she knew that "neither raptures, nor revelations, nor gifts granted to a soul make it perfect, but rather the intimate union of the soul with God. These gifts are merely ornaments of the soul, but constitute neither its essence nor its perfection. My sanctity and perfection consist in the close union of my will with the will of God." Jesus let her learn that what He wanted from His creatures was trust, while many souls, even those spiritually very advanced, did not fully trust Him because they did not know His mercy. The sins which hurt Him most were the sins of mistrust, He told Sister Faustina. "This mistrust of My goodness hurts me very much. If My death has not convinced you of My love, what will? "

The mystery of God's merciful love shaped and transformed her entire life, not only in relation to God but her fellow humans, who in the light of this truth were God's beloved children, redeemed by the blood of His Son and meant to enjoy eternal life with Him. Jesus Himself instructed her how and in what spirit she was to practise mercy. He wanted her always and everywhere to show mercy through word, deed, or prayer. He taught her that spiritual mercy had a greater value, for which neither permission nor money was needed. He said that the mercy administered to people was to derive from love for Him, and that it was Man's greatest asset on earth. He explained that "even the strongest faith was of no avail without works [of mercy]" and that all people, even one's enemies, were to be loved. Sister Faustina put all of Jesus' words into practice, and there were plenty of occasions for this. One evening she returned to her cell so exhausted that she could hardly prepare for bed. Meanwhile another sister asked her to fetch her some warm water. Although the mud was ankle-deep and she was extremely tired, she took up the water-jug and went out into another building to carry out the request.

Jesus took the opportunity to tell her of the value of every good work. "Approach each of the sisters with the same love with which you approach Me; and whatever you do for them, you do it for Me."

Excited with God's loving mercy, she wanted to turn into mercy and be its living reflection. "O my Jesus," she entreated in prayer, "each of Your saints reflects one of Your virtues; I desire to reflect Your compassionate heart, full of mercy; I want to glorify it. Let Your mercy, O Jesus, be impressed upon my heart and soul like a seal, and this will be my badge in this and the future life." Instructed by the Master's words and example, she endeavoured to follow Him faithfully even unto the sacrifice of her life. On Maundy Thursday 1934 she entered in her diary an act of self-sacrifice for sinners, especially those who have lost hope in God's mercy. In this act she bound herself to accept with absolute submission to the will of God all the suffering, fears and anxieties of those who are far from God, and in return she offered them all the comforts she had received in her exceptionally intimate communion with God. In this manner day by day she was gradually transforming into mercy: her eyes, ears, tongue, hands and feet, and above all her heart were full of an active love of her neighbours. She was able to make use of each and every opportunity to increase in love, as she realised that "Great love can change small things into great ones, and it is only love which lends value to our actions." In the life of Sister Faustina mercy was not limited to occasional acts of showing love of her fellow humans, it gradually turned into her entire lifestyle.

She drew the strength for the transformation of her life into mercy from daily Holy Communion. She soon discovered that this was a privileged space for the meeting of Man with his Divine Maker and that it had the power to sanctify human life. Not only through faith but also through mystical experience did she learn the reality of every Mass and the greatness of this gift of Divine mercy for humans. "If the angels were capable of envy," she wrote, "they would envy us for two things: one is the receiving of Holy Communion, and the other is suffering." Holy Communion gives mankind an opportunity for closer union with God than what the angels have in heaven. It is not for them that the Son of God becomes Bread. Aware of this gift, she tried to prepare for Holy Mass as fully as she could and participated in it by offering herself and her communion up with Jesus for the salvation of sinners, and to put into practice throughout the day the demands made by the Eucharist to become bread for one's brethren. The way she prepared to receive

Holy Communion is instructive, because it shows the richness of her spiritual life and her personal bond with Jesus. On one occasion she would receive Him as her King, another time as her Bridegroom, Love, Redeemer, Source of Mercy, Lord... But each time the meeting was accompanied by an intense longing to unite with Him in love and to fully imitate Him, unto transformation and immolation as another sacrifice. On receiving Holy Communion she entreated, "Jesus, transform me into another host! I want to be a living host for You. You are the great and all-powerful Lord; You can grant me this favour. And the Lord answered me, 'You are a living host, pleasing to the Heavenly Father. But reflect: What is a host? A sacrifice. And so...?' O my Jesus, I understand the meaning of 'host,' the meaning of sacrifice. I desire to be before Your Majesty a living host; that is, a living sacrifice that daily burns in your honour."

Her love of the Eucharist was expressed also in the adoration of the Blessed Sacrament. She spent all her free time at the feet of the Lord hidden in the consecrated Bread. Here she sought enlightenment and strength. Jesus of the Eucharist was everything for her. "All that is good in me," she wrote towards the end of her life, "is due to Holy Communion, I owe everything to it. I feel that this holy fire has transformed me completely."

8.

New tasks

The joy brought by the accomplishment of Jesus' requests, the painting of the picture and its display for public veneration on the first Sunday after Easter, the envisaged Feast of Divine Mercy, did not last long. Already in May 1935 Sister Faustina felt intuitively that there would be new tasks which she was very anxious about. When once instead of praying she started reading a religious book, she heard an inner voice, "You will prepare the world for My final coming." These words stirred her deeply, and although she pretended not to have heard them she understood them but for the time being did not tell anyone of them.

On the Feast of Pentecost, 9 June 1935, in the evening, when she was in the garden, Jesus gave her a new task: "By your entreaties, you and your companions shall obtain mercy for yourselves and for the world." Like the biblical prophets, she started enumerating her inadequacies and excusing herself that she was not capable of accomplishing this work. Jesus paid no attention to this and did not withdraw His directive, but encouraged her, saying, "Do not fear; I myself will make up for everything that is lacking in you." But she wasn't sure she had understood His words correctly, that she was to found a new congregation, neither had she been told explicitly to inform her confessor of this, so for the next twenty days she remained silent. Only during a discussion with her spiritual director Father Sopoćko did she disclose that "God demands that there be a Congregation which will proclaim the mercy of God to the world and, by its prayers, obtain it for the world." During this conversation she saw Jesus, who confirmed that this was His will, saying, "I desire there be such a Congregation." Her repeated protests that she felt unable to meet such a demand were of no avail. On the next day during Mass she saw Jesus, who yet again said that He wanted such a work founded as soon as possible. In a mystical experience after Holy Communion she received a blessing for the task from the Holy Trinity. This proved such an encouragement that it seemed to her nothing would be too difficult, and in an inner act she agreed to carry out

God's will although she knew it would mean great suffering for her.

Initially Sister Faustina thought that she was to leave her Congregation and found a contemplative order in which she and her companions were to beg for mercy for themselves and for the world. She asked St. Ignatius Loyola, founder of a religious order and patron of the Congregation, to help her discern the will of God. He told her that the rule could be adapted to her Congregation as well, but his meaning was not clear to her. She could not see how these new tasks, preaching and praying for God's mercy, could be reconciled with the Congregation's mission hitherto. A spell of great suffering started for her, a period of passive nights of the spirit, in which her mind and will were purged even of those of the ordinary human attributes which were an obstacle to her intimate union with God. On the one hand she felt an urgency to complete the task, on the other she was restrained by obedience. "Why are you afraid?" she heard from Jesus, "Do you think that I will not have enough omnipotence to support you?" These words encouraged her to take action, she was ready to leave her Congregation and found a new one, but for the time being she did not have the express consent for this either from her superiors, or from her confessor, or from Archbishop Romuald Jałbrzykowski, who advised her to have the entreaties for Divine Mercy conducted in her own Congregation and wait until Jesus arranged the right circumstances for the fulfilment of His will.

After confession with the Archbishop, on Friday, 13 September 1935, Sister Faustina had a vision in her cell of an Angel who was sent down by God to punish the earth. Seeing this sign of God's wrath, she started begging the Angel to hold off a while for the world to do penance, but when she stood before the majesty of the Holy Trinity she did not dare repeat her plea. But in her soul she felt the power of Jesus' grace and started to entreat God in the words which she heard in her heart and which later became part of the Chaplet to the Divine Mercy. Then she saw the powerlessness of the Angel, who could not administer the just punishment for the sins of mankind. On the next day when she entered the chapel Jesus instructed her once more how she was to say the prayer on an ordinary rosary. "First of all, you will say one Our Father and Hail Mary and the I Believe in God. Then on the Our Father beads you will say the following words: 'Eternal Father, I offer You the Body and Blood, Soul and Divinity of Your dearly beloved Son, Our Lord Jesus Christ, in atonement for our sins and those of the whole world.' On the Hail Mary beads you will say the following words: 'For the sake of His sorrowful Passion have mercy on us and on the whole world,' In conclusion, three times you will recite these words: 'Holy God, Holy Mighty One, Holy Immortal One, have mercy on us and on the whole world.'" This is the prayer for the appeasing of God's wrath.

In the next visions Jesus made great promises to Sister Faustina in connection with the trustful reciting of the chaplet. He promised the grace of a happy and peaceful death not only to those who say the chaplet, but also those at whose deathbed others will say the chaplet. "Even the most hardened sinner who says the chaplet only once will receive grace from My infinite mercy," He said. "It pleases Me to grant everything they ask of Me when they say the chaplet." These and other promises Jesus made would be fulfilled only if the practices He had recommended were accompanied by an inner attitude of trust in God combined with an active love of one's neighbour.

In the Vilnian period Jesus returned to the issue of the establishment of the Feast of Divine Mercy in the Church. He reminded Sister Faustina that He wanted it celebrated on the first Sunday after Easter, for souls were still being lost despite His bitter Passion. That day was to be the refuge for all souls, especially the poor sinners. "On that day the very depths of My tender mercy are open," He promised, "I pour out a whole ocean of graces upon those souls who come to the fount of My mercy. The soul that goes to Confession and receives Holy Communion shall obtain complete forgiveness of sins and punishment. On that day are open all the divine floodgates through which graces flow. Let no soul fear to come to Me, even though its sins be as scarlet." Priests were to preach sermons on God's loving mercy for Man and make their hearts trust in Him, thereby enabling them to draw on the fountainhead of Divine Mercy. "Mankind will not have peace until it turns with trust to My mercy," He told Sister Faustina.

Instructed by Jesus not to do anything without the consent of her confessors and superiors, Sister Faustina stayed in the Congregation and with the help of her spiritual director tried to interpret God's intentions. Recurrent visions of a new congregation and its convents urged her and her spiritual adviser to diagnose the will of God and take action. Visions concerning the location of this new congregation came several times: once it was a small convent with twelve sisters next to a small church; another time it was a windowless building with no doors; on yet another occasion it was a huge edifice inhabited by people dressed like laity, but the spirit was radically evangelical. Sister Faustina did not fully understand these visions, nonetheless she and Father Sopoćko visited a property at Number 12 in the ulica św. Anny, Wilno (Vilnius) to see whether it was the place in the vision. The buildings there resembled what she had seen in the vision, but despite efforts she did not succeed in obtaining the property for the envisaged new convent.

During the eight-day retreat she made in Kraków in October 1935 Sister Faustina discussed the question of a new congregation with Father Józef Andrasz. For a whole day before making her confession she fought an arduous spiritual battle. She felt that God had forsaken her, that she was a weak human menaced by grave temptations. Her mind and heart were assailed by a barrage of questions: "why should I leave this convent where I am loved by the sisters and superiors, where life is so tranquil; where I am bound by perpetual vows and carry out my duties without difficulty; why should I listen to the voice of my conscience, why follow an inspiration coming from who knows where; wouldn't it be better to carry on like all the other sisters? Perhaps the Lord's words could be stifled, not taken heed of; maybe God will not demand an account of them on the day of judgement. Where will this inner voice lead me? If I follow it, what tremendous difficulties, tribulations and adversities are in store for me. I fear the future, and am agonising in the present." Father Andrasz advised caution and recommended committing the matter to her prayers. In his opinion the idea itself seemed good but he considered that these were only the initial stages of the work God intended to carry out. That is why he counselled her not to do anything on her own but confide in her spiritual director and carry out his recommendations in a spirit of obedience. This would prevent her from going wrong.

Initially believing Jesus wanted her to found a contemplative order, Sister Faustina compiled an abstract of its rule, with a very austere lifestyle, strict silence and complete isolation from the world, so that the sisters could be as if pure, immolated victims for God, effectively pleading for His mercy for all people, but especially for sinners, and for priests and religious. The characteristic feature of this spiritual community was to be a self-sacrificing love of God and every soul. She wrote in the abstract, "As God makes us sharers in His mercy and even more than that, dispensers of that mercy, we should therefore have great love for each soul, from the elect to the soul that does not yet know God. By prayer and mortification, we will reach the most uncivilised countries, paving the way for the missionaries. We will bear in mind that as a soldier on the front line cannot hold out long without support from the rear forces that do not actually take part in the fighting but provide all his needs, so too the missionary has all his needs provided for by prayer."

In August 1934 Sister Faustina's health suddenly deteriorated and she found herself at death's door. But after she had received the Sacrament of the Sick and had been examined by a doctor there was a radical improvement. She was sent back to work in the garden, and had a few of the most troublesome charges to help her. But there was so much work that her ailing strength could not cope with it all. Further medical tests revealed she was suffering from a fairly advanced stage of tuberculosis. In this situation Mother General decided to transfer Sister Faustina to Walendów, thereafter to nearby Derdy, and finally to Kraków.

9.

Dark nights

Along with the new tasks, there now came a second stage of anguishing purification known as the passive nights of the spirit. The background to and instrument whereby God effected this in Sister Faustina's soul was the work for the implementation of the concept of a new congregation. At first Sister Faustina thought that Jesus wanted her to leave her mother Congregation and found a contemplative order. It was with this in mind that on 21 March 1936 she left Vilnius.

On her way to Walendów she stopped at Warsaw, where she had the opportunity to discuss the matter with Mother General Michaela Moraczewska, in whom she had always been able to confide. Having listened to Sister Faustina, Mother General said that for the time being it was God's will that she should stay in her Congregation, where she had made her perpetual vows, but she also expressed an opinion that the work of mercy which Jesus was entrusting to her must be very beautiful, since it was meeting with so much opposition from Satan. However, she advised her not to hurry with the foundation of a new congregation, for if the idea indeed came from God, then it would be accomplished in its time.

During her stay of several weeks at Walendów and Derdy Sister Faustina's spiritual suffering became more aggravated. Under the strain of internal pressure, during her quarterly confession she declared that she could not wait any longer but wanted to leave the Congregation and start the work. But she did not receive the consent of her confessor, who considered this idea illusory. This was heightened by the suffering of uniting with Jesus in His Passion. In a letter to Father Sopoćko she wrote, "I feel an extraordinary interior force which drives me to action, and, because of this, an indescribable torment afflicts my soul; yet I would not exchange this agony for all the treasures of the world, for it is caused by God's love." In the tremendous suffering her only thought was to carry out God's will as faithfully as possible, which was for her the light and everyday sustenance, strength in the surmounting of natural weakness and accomplishing the tasks entrusted her. "O My Jesus, Master and Director," she prayed, "strengthen and enlighten me in these difficult moments of my life; I expect no help from people; all my hope is in You. I feel alone in the face of Your demands, O Lord. Despite the fears and qualms of my nature, I am fulfilling Your holy will and desire to fulfil it as faithfully as possible throughout my life and in my death." In the great suffering which was piercing her soul it was to God, in prayer and in confession, not to fellow humans that she turned for help.

After a few weeks' stay at Walendów she went to the Congregation's house at Derdy, which was just a kilometre away. Here she cooked for the small group of sisters and over thirty charges. "Her kitchen help," Sister Serafina Kukulska recalled, "was a girl with a very difficult character, a convert, whom no-one ever wanted to work with. But with Sister Faustina the girl changed and was never the same again. That was the quiet, godly influence Sister Faustina had on sinful souls." There was not much work for her to do at Derdy, and Sister Faustina felt as if staying in this house was almost like a holiday. In the afternoons she was to have two hours of sleep, and could perform some of her spiritual exercises in the nearby wood, breathing in the pure and wholesome air. She felt that here she could recuperate her highly taxed physical strength. But soon she had to leave for Kraków, where there were better medical facilities for the treatment of tuberculosis. She also hoped that coming to that house would mean the final accomplishing of God's plans concerning the foundation of a new congregation.

Although she had already realised that the new "congregation" would be a great work in the Church, comprising men's and women's congregations as well as lay associations, as she wrote to Father Sopoćko in April 1936, she was still convinced that her role in this was to found a contemplative order. On arriving in Kraków she met with Father Andrasz, who advised her to keep praying and exercising acts of self-mortification until the Feast of the Sacred Heart, when he would give her an answer to this question. However, under heavy inner pressure, Sister Faustina did not wait until the feast-day but told Father Andrasz during her weekly confession that she had decided to leave the Congregation. Her Cracovian spiritual director observed that since she had taken the decision she would be taking the full responsibility on herself. At first she was happy to be leaving, but on the next day was overwhelmed by darkness and felt she had lost God's presence, so she decided to put off this move a little until her next meeting with her confessor.

At first Mother General had not consented to her leaving the Congregation and had warned Sister

Faustina to beware of delusions and imprudent moves, she had "locked her away with Jesus in the tabernacle" so that the decisions she took should comply with the will of God. She had asked for prayer and a sign from God that this was indeed His will. But now that she was travelling to Kraków for a visitation she decided to ask the opinion of the sisters who were general councillors. They were in favour of the possibility of Sister Faustina being granted permission to leave the Congregation if she still wanted to take this step. On 4 May 1937, in the first days of the visitation, Sister Faustina spoke with Mother General and asked whether she had had any light on the question of her departure from the Congregation. Mother General replied, "Until the present, Sister, I have always restrained you, but now I leave you complete freedom to choose to do as you wish; you can leave the Congregation or you can stay." Sister Faustina decided to leave and straightaway write to the Holy Father to dispense her from her vows. But yet again she was overwhelmed by such darkness that she returned to Mother General's room to tell her of her tribulation and struggle.

This was her last attempt to leave the Congregation, but the spiritual struggle continued. She wrote in her diary, "No-one can understand or comprehend, nor can I myself describe, my torments. But there can be no sufferings greater than this. The sufferings of the martyrs are not greater because, at such times, death would be a relief for me. There is nothing to which I can compare these sufferings, this endless agony of the soul." Her soul was being purified in the crucible of spiritual battle. Her intellect, will, memory, emotions and all her senses were submitting to God more and more harmoniously and preparing her soul for full union with Him. God never sends suffering that is unbearable, she used to say, for the greater the suffering, the greater God's grace. In the darkness of the passive nights God was granting her moments of respite and great joy. "I suddenly saw the Lord Jesus," she described one of these moments, "who spoke these words to me: 'Now I know it is not for the graces or gifts that you love Me, but because My will is dearer to you than life. That is why I am uniting Myself with you so intimately as with no other creature.' At that moment, Jesus disappeared. My soul was filled with the presence of God. I know that the gaze of the Mighty One rests upon me. I plunged myself completely in the joy that flows from God."

Father Sopoćko, her Vilnian spiritual director, also contributed to the deciphering of God's will regarding a new congregation. Father Andrasz directed Sister Faustina to him, and she kept him fully informed in letters describing all her actions. Father Sopoćko also sought the advice of Archbishop Jałbrzykowski, and all the time advised her to be very cautious in all her external actions. In a letter he wrote, "God does not require haste from His servants, but prudent and discreet actions. Masters of the spiritual life say that where there is haste, there is no divine action. That is why we too must not act needleessly with haste; let us curb our interior impulsions, asking God for assistance, that He might arrange the conditions for action. For it is better to do nothing than to do something badly, or to thwart God's plans through haste without discretion. I see God's action in this whole matter and that is precisely why I do not advise you to rush, as everything happens in its time. What God has determined will happen, even if the greatest obstacles were to mount, for who is able to oppose the Creator?"

Reassured by her Vilnian spiritual director, Sister Faustina patiently submitted to the decrees of Providence, and above all was making progress on her road to full union with God. She realised that the work God was asking her to carry out could be conducted in a different way to what she had thought hitherto. God had shown her that He was pleased with what had been achieved so far, while the problems they were encountering only confirmed the fact that God found the work pleasing. "I don't have a shadow of a doubt," she wrote to Father Sopoćko. "It is the explicit will of God. Through us God initiated His work, and it is not for us to know who will complete it; but we should do what is in our power and nothing more." In this situation she stopped worrying about obtaining permission to found a new convent, its location, the recruitment and formation of appropriate candidates, and instead concentrated on prayer and the sacrifices she was making in this intention.

In June 1937 she made a record in her diary of the final shape of the work which was one but had three hues. The first hue comprised the souls separated off from the world, which would burn in immolation before the Divine Majesty, begging for mercy for the whole world and prepare it for the Second Coming of Christ. The second hue would be the active congregations, which would combine prayer with acts of mercy and make the merciful love of God present in an egoistic world. The third hue could be made up of all the people who by daily acts of mercy on behalf of their neighbours, by their words and prayers and for the love of Jesus would fulfil the tasks of this work.

The achievement of this objective not only brought Sister Faustina the greatest amount of suffering, but also led her to full union with Jesus, to what is generally referred to as mystical betrothal and mystical marriage. Purified in the passive nights, the powers of her soul no longer put up any opposition: her reason and will longed only for God and whatever He longed for. The Lord brought her into the world of an ever closer union with Him, preparing her for the next grace, preceded by a mystical experience of the Holy Trinity. This is how she described it in her diary:

"On one occasion, God's presence pervaded my whole being, and my mind was mysteriously enlightened in respect to His Essence. He allowed me to understand His interior life. In spirit, I saw the Three Divine Persons, but Their Essence was One. He is One, and One only, but in Three Persons; none of Them is either greater or smaller; there is no difference in either beauty or sanctity, for They are One. They are absolutely One. His Love transported me into this knowledge and united me with Himself. When I was united to One, I was equally united to the Second and to the Third in such a way that when we are united with One, by that very fact, we are equally united to the two Persons in the same way as with the One. Their will is One, one God, though in Three Persons. When one of the Three Persons communicates with a soul, by the power of that one will, it finds itself united with the Three Persons and is inundated in the happiness flowing from the Most Holy Trinity, the same happiness that nourishes the saints... In these moments, my soul experienced such divine delights that I find this difficult to express."

After this experience of God she heard the words of Jesus, "I want you to be my spouse." She wondered what this might mean. She had made her perpetual vows, so she felt that this must be a new, extraordinary grace. As she was pondering it, she alternated between bliss and fainting for longing for God, but in the fainting she preserved a clear, enlightened mind. She was thankful for this tremendous grace which enabled her to be in communion with Jesus. "Jesus, Your Name is my delight," she told Him, "I have a presentiment of my Beloved from afar, and my languishing soul rests in His embrace; I don't know how to live without Him. I would rather be with Him in afflictions and suffering than without Him in the greatest heavenly delights."

After the mystical betrothal came the time for mystical marriage. "At that moment I was transfixed by the Divine light and felt I belonged exclusively to God, and I experienced the supreme spiritual freedom, the like of which I had never dreamed of before." Now only a very thin veil of faith separated her from the union with God to which the saints accede in heaven.

10.

I send you out to the whole world

In the Cracovian convent Sister Faustina received the rest of the prophetic mission which started with the vision of Jesus she had in Płock, in which He told her to have a picture painted and establish the Feast of the Divine Mercy on the first Sunday after Easter. In October 1937 Jesus gave Sister Faustina another form of worship of the Divine Mercy. He asked her to hold the moment of His death on the cross in veneration. "At three o'clock, implore My mercy, especially for sinners; and, if only for a brief moment, immerse yourself in My Passion, particularly in My abandonment at the moment of agony. This is the hour of great mercy for the whole world." In His next apparition He gave the details for this type of worship. He asked Sister Faustina to do the Stations of the Cross at the hour of His death, but if duty prevented this, to come to the chapel for a short moment of prayer before the Blessed Sacrament, and if even that was out of the question, to devote a brief moment to prayer wherever she was. He made a promise that He would bestow graces on all who offered up trustful prayer to Him at three o'clock in the afternoon on the merit of His Passion. These graces would be granted to the petitioners and all for whom they prayed, naturally provided the grace asked for was in agreement with the will of God, that is good for that person from the perspective of eternity. "In this hour you can obtain everything for yourself and for others for the asking; it was the hour of grace for the whole world – mercy triumphed over justice," He assured Sister Faustina.

Sister Faustina continued to keep her diary in Kraków, recording not only Jesus' words and her extraordinary mystical experiences, but also deeply moving contemplation on the mystery of Divine Mercy. She wrote passages describing God's goodness in the creation of the angels, the world, and Man, in the incarnation and birth of the Son of God, in the work of redemption and in His Church, especially in the Sacraments, and in His intention for mankind to share in the life of God on earth and for all eternity. She also made a record of some fine dialogues between various persons in different spiritual conditions and the merciful Lord. In these accounts she showed God's unfathomable grace and love for the suffering, sinners, those in despair, those in search of perfection, and those who have achieved perfection. The over eight-month period of illness and two spells in Prądnik Hospital was a good time for writing, and a major part of her spiritual writings was done in Kraków. This was also when she underlined the words Jesus had said, as instructed by her Vilnian spiritual adviser.

Jesus' request that she proclaim His Mercy to the world occurs time and again throughout the diary. It was an exhortation Sister Faustina heard many times: "Write down these words, ...tell the world about My mercy and My love. The flames of mercy are burning Me. I desire to pour them out on human souls. Oh, what pain they cause me when they do not want to accept them! My daughter, do whatever is within your power to spread devotion to My mercy. I will make up for what you lack. Tell aching mankind to snuggle close to My merciful Heart, and I will fill it with peace. Tell all people, My daughter, that I am Love and Mercy itself."

This task was of special importance, since Jesus attached such great promises to it. He said, "Souls who spread the honour of My mercy I shield through their entire life as a tender mother her infant, and at the hour of death I will not be a Judge for them, but the merciful Saviour." He promised special graces to priests who preached the truth of God's merciful love for mankind. He would bless their words and endow them with such great power that even the most hardened of sinners would repent.

Sister Faustina fulfilled this mission not only by the witness of her own life and the writing of her diary, in which she revealed God's extraordinary merciful love for each human being, but also through her everyday relations with her neighbours. "One day," Sister Eufemia Traczyńska recalled, "when we were peeling apples at work in the bakery Sister Faustina came in. We were sitting on a bench and she came up from behind, put her arms around our shoulders and put her head between our heads. Sister Amelia, who had a very sensitive conscience, asked her, 'Sister, how come, when you try so hard but over the week you still commit such a lot of sins. What can you do about it?' 'Well,' said Sister Faustina, 'if you have a yard then what with walking across it all week it'll get dirty, but come Saturday you sweep it and clean it up and it's spotless. So when we go to confession our souls are spotless and we have nothing to worry about. Jesus will take care of it.'" In her everyday contacts Sister Faustina was able to interpret life's troubles in a spirit of living faith and see

God's goodness in everything. She would often tell the sisters and charges about God's love of mankind and about the tremendous value of doing good to one's neighbour. One day passing by the chapel she said to Sister Damiana Ziółek, "I heard that Jesus said that at the Last Judgement He would judge people only on their mercy, for God is Mercy, so by doing or failing to do merciful deeds you are casting a verdict on yourself."

As Jesus told her, His request that God's merciful love for mankind be preached is the last recourse for many souls, which are being lost notwithstanding His bitter Passion. It is also the means to establish peace in human hearts and between nations: "Mankind will not have peace until it turns with trust to My mercy." And it is to prepare the world for His second coming. "That God is infinitely merciful, no-one can deny. He desires everyone to know this before He comes again as Judge. He wants souls to come to know Him first as King of Mercy," Sister Faustina wrote in her diary.

Our Lady, the best of mothers and mistress of the spiritual life, faithfully accompanied Sister Faustina and spoke to her on the prophetic mission entrusted her. She taught her how to live in communion with God in her own soul, to love His will and her neighbour, to accept suffering and bear her daily cross; she comforted and encouraged her; she patiently explained things beyond human reasoning. The visions and words of Our Lady were in absolute harmony with the prophetic mission Jesus had entrusted to His Secretary "In the morning, during meditation," Sister Faustina recorded, "God's presence enveloped me in a special way, as I saw the immeasurable greatness of God and, at the same time, His condescension to His creatures. Then I saw the Mother of God, who said to me, 'Oh, how pleasing to God is the soul that follows faithfully the inspirations of His grace! I gave the Saviour to the world; as for you, you have to speak to the world about His great mercy and prepare the world for the Second Coming of Him who will come, not as a merciful Saviour, but as a just Judge. Oh, how terrible is that day! Determined is the day of justice, the day of divine wrath. The angels tremble before it. Speak to souls about this great mercy while it is still the time for mercy. If you keep silent now, you will be answering for a great number of souls on that terrible day. Fear nothing. Be faithful to the end. I am in empathy with you.'"

The mystery of Divine Mercy took up the central position in Sister Faustina's life and apostolic work. In accordance with the words of Jesus and His Mother, not only was she to live by it herself, reflecting it in her heart and works, but she was also to let the whole world learn of it. It was yet another task which seemed to transcend her capabilities. After all, she lived in a convent and was only a simple nun performing prosaic duties; she had neither extensive relations with other people nor any opportunities to disseminate this message in the world at large. But it was to her that Jesus addressed these amazing words: "In the Old Covenant I sent prophets wielding thunderbolts to My people. Today I am sending you with My mercy to the people of the whole world. I do not want to punish aching mankind, but I desire to heal it, pressing it to My Merciful Heart. I use punishment when they themselves force Me to do so; My hand is reluctant to take hold of the sword of justice. Before the Day of Justice I am sending the Day of Mercy." She firmly believed all He said would happen, though sometimes she had no idea as to how it would come about. However, she knew that the convent chapel at Łagiewniki in Kraków would become the shrine for the worship of the Divine Mercy. She told Sister Bożenna Pniewska, who regretted that the Łagiewniki chapel was available only for the sisters and their charges, "There will soon come a time when the convent gate will be wide open and people will come here to pray to the Divine Mercy."

11.

*To the House
of the Merciful Father*

Tuberculosis, which had not been diagnosed until her stay in Vilnius, was ravaging Sister Faustina's body. It had attacked not only the respiratory system but also the alimentary canal. Her superiors sent her for treatment to a sanatorium in the municipal health institution in Kraków. Her first period of treatment lasted nearly four months from December 1936 (with a break for Christmas). Already on her third day there she had evidence of the efficacy of the Chaplet to the Divine Mercy Jesus had given her. She woke up during the night and realised that a soul was asking her for prayer. When she entered the ward next day she saw that one of the patients was dying and heard that the agony had begun during the night at the hour when she had woken up. In her soul she heard Jesus' words: "Say the chaplet which I taught you."

She fetched her rosary, knelt by the dying person's bedside and started saying the chaplet with all the powers of her spirit, asking Jesus to fulfil the promise He had made regarding the chaplet. Suddenly the dying person opened her eyes, looked at Sister Faustina, and died with an extraordinary calm on her face. And Jesus said, "At the hour of death, I will defend as My own glory every soul that says this chaplet; or when others say it for a dying person, the indulgence is the same. When this chaplet is said by the bedside of a dying person, God's anger is placated, and unfathomable mercy envelops the soul, and the very depths of My tender mercy will be moved for the sake of the sorrowful Passion of My Son."

That is how Sister Faustina's hospital ministry for the dying started. Though seriously ill herself, often so ill that she had to leave Mass, she always noticed others, who needed help. And when her superior forbade her these visits to the bedsides of the dying on account of her own poor health, she would offer up her prayers and acts of obedience for them, which as Jesus had taught her meant more in His eyes than great deeds undertaken wilfully. She also helped not only those who were dying in the sanatorium, but thanks to the gift of bilocation also those dying in another part of the hospital or even hundreds of miles away. This happened on several occasions, when a relative or one of the sisters, or even someone she had never known was dying. For the spirit space does not exist. She was grateful to God for allowing her in this way to bring relief and assistance to the dying.

During her first hospitalisation she suffered much because for nearly the first three weeks she had no access to confession, as when the time came for confession in the convent, she either had to stay in bed or was on her way to the hospital. With these things on her mind as she lay in her room, she burst out crying. "This afternoon," she wrote in her diary, "Father Andrasz came into my room and sat down to hear my confession. Beforehand, we did not exchange a single word. I was delighted because I was extremely anxious to go to confession. As usual, I unveiled my whole soul. Father gave a reply to each little detail. I felt unusually happy to be able to say everything as I did. For penance, he gave me the Litany of the Holy Name of Jesus. When I wanted to tell him of the difficulty I have in saying this litany, he rose and began to give me absolution. Suddenly his figure became diffused with a great light, and I saw it was not Father A., but Jesus. His garments were bright as snow, and He disappeared immediately. At first, I was a little uneasy, but after a while a kind of peace entered my soul; and I took note of the fact that Jesus heard the confession in the same way that confessors do; and yet something was wondrously transpiring in my heart during this confession. I couldn't at first understand what it signified."

When Christmas came Dr. Adam Sielberg allowed Sister Faustina to return to the convent to spend the holy time with the other nuns. Sister Kajetana Bartkowiak came in a carriage to collect her. Sister Faustina was very excited, and on the way home had the following evangelical thoughts: "As we were riding through the city I imagined it was the town of Bethlehem. As I watched all those people hurrying about, I thought: who is meditating today, in recollection and silence, on this inconceivable mystery? O pure Virgin, You are travelling today, and so am I. I feel that today's journey has its symbolism. ...O my Mother, how ardently I desire that You give me the Infant Jesus during the Midnight Mass." Our Lady made her wish come true. During Midnight Mass the Divine presence transfixed her. She saw the Virgin and Child with St. Joseph. "My daughter, Faustina," Our Lady said to her, "take this most precious Treasure," and gave her little Jesus. As she was holding the Baby Jesus, her soul was experiencing such sublime ecstasy that, as she noted, she could not describe it.

Straight after Christmas she returned to hospital, to her "hermitage" as she called the room in the tuberculosis ward. She tried to perform all her spiritual exercises, even the retreat, just as if she were in the convent. She made resolutions, asked her superior for permission for additional mortifications, and availed herself of the daily administration of the Sacrament by the chaplain who said Mass in the chapel next to the ward, and in her leisure time made new entries in her diary. Her life passed in tranquil awareness of God living in her soul. He was the source of her happiness and strength. He also visited her on numerous occasions in her room, to strengthen her resolution and give her courage to accept the suffering of illness and to carry out her prophetic mission.

News of Father Sopoćko's efforts to disseminate the devotion to Divine Mercy, of which he informed her in his letters, and the first brochure with prayers to the Divine Mercy Jesus had given her made her very happy. Thanks to Father Sopoćko's endeavours the brochure was printed in Kraków. One day, as she took up a copy with the picture of the Merciful Jesus, she spontaneously uttered the following words: "Jesus, Eternal Love, I live for You, I die for You and I want to become united with You." Then she saw the Lord unbelievably radiant. He looked at her graciously and said, "My daughter, I too came down from heaven out of love for you. I lived for you, I died for you and I created the heavens for you." And Jesus clasped her to His heart, warming her soul with encouragement to bear more suffering.

Along with great physical and spiritual suffering there were also vast graces, which Sister Faustina did not divulge to anyone except her confessors. But occasionally someone was a witness to them. "One day I went to Prądnik to visit her," Sister Kajetana Bartkowiak recollected, "I knocked on the door. She always used to say, 'Come in, please,' but this time there was no answer though I knocked and knocked. I thought she must be in her room and lying in bed, as she was ill, so I opened the door and went in. Then I saw her all different, changed, and levitating over the bed, gazing into the distance as if she were looking at something there. I stood next to the bed-side cabinet on which there was a little altar set up and was overwhelmed with terror, but a moment later she came round and said, 'Ah, Sister, you've come, I'm glad, do come in.'" Informed of this, Mother Superior Irena Krzyżanowska forbade her to speak about it, and this is how Sister Faustina's extraordinary spiritual life was kept secret.

The first stage of her hospital treatment ended in March 1937. Her health slightly improved, Sister

Faustina returned to Łagiewniki Convent. But already in April she suffered a relapse. In July her superiors sent her to the Congregation's house in the spa resort of Rabka, but the sharp mountain climate was not good for Sister Faustina, she felt worse and had to leave after thirteen days. But she took with her St. Joseph's assurance that he was very much in favour of the work of Mercy entrusted her by the Lord. He promised her his special help and protection, but asked her every day to say three prayers and the *Memorare*, a prayer which the Congregation said in honour of St. Joseph. From henceforth Sister Faustina knew that she was supported in the carrying out of the mission not only by the Blessed Virgin but also St. Joseph. Other saints and angels, whose company and assistance she had often enjoyed, also lent a helping hand.

On her return from Rabka Sister Faustina was given a lighter duty, in the entrance lodge, than her previous job in the garden. Here she had plenty of opportunities to perform acts of mercy to various people – vagrants, the unemployed, hungry children – who called at the lodge gate asking for assistance. In each of them she tried to discern Jesus Himself and out of love for Him did good works for all of them. One day "a poor young man, emaciated, barefoot and bareheaded" appeared at the lodge, as Sister Faustina described the incident, "with his clothes in tatters ...frozen because the day was cold and rainy. He asked for something hot to eat. So I went to the kitchen but found nothing there for the poor. But, after searching around for some time, I found some soup, which I reheated and into which I crumbled some bread, and I gave it to the poor young man, who ate it. As I was taking the bowl from him, he gave me to know that He was the Lord of heaven and earth. When I saw Him as He was, He vanished from my sight. When I went back in and reflected on what had happened at the gate, I heard these words in my soul: 'My daughter, the blessings of the poor who bless Me as they leave this gate have reached My ears. And your compassion, within the bounds of obedience, has pleased Me, and this is why I came down from My throne – to taste the fruits of your mercy.'"

The first months of 1938 saw a further deterioration in Sister Faustina's health, and her superiors decided to send her to Prądnik Hospital again after Easter. The Sister Servants of the Most Sacred Heart, who worked as nurses in the hospital, prepared a room for her, but in the evening one of them informed her that she would not have Holy Communion the next day because she was exhausted. "In the morning I made my meditation," she noted in her diary, "and prepared for Holy Communion, even though I was not to receive the Lord Jesus. When my love and desire had reached a high degree, I saw at my bedside a Seraph, who gave me Holy Communion, saying these words, 'Behold the Lord of Angels.' When I received the Lord, my spirit was submerged in the love of God and in amazement. This was repeated for thirteen days, although I was never sure he would bring me Holy Communion the next day. Yet, I put my trust completely in the goodness of God."

She continued to make entries in her diary almost to the end of June. She noted down the words of Jesus, her prayers, contemplation and the more important events, including her last three-day retreat given her by Jesus Himself before the Feast of Pentecost. Every day He gave her a subject for contemplation and points for meditation. He preached conferences on spiritual struggle, sacrifice, prayer, and mercy. Sister Faustina was to contemplate His love for her and love of one's neighbour. Under such direction her mind had no problems with comprehending all the mysteries of faith, and her heart burned with the living flame of love. On the Feast of Pentecost she renewed her religious vows. Her soul was in special communion with the Holy Spirit, whose inspiration filled it with indescribable ecstasy, and her heart was flooded with thanksgiving for such vast graces.

The other sisters who visited her in hospital noticed her radiant happiness. "I often visited her," Sister Serafina Kukulska recalled, "and always found her cheerful, even happy, and sometimes as if radiant, but she never disclosed the secret of her happiness. She was very happy in Prądnik and never complained that she was suffering. The doctor, the nurses, the patients – they were all very good to her." Sister Felicja Żakowiecka visited Sister Faustina twice a week. During these visits she spoke with Dr. Adam Sielberg on Sister Faustina's condition. The doctor said it was very bad. Sister Felicja was surprised that the doctor allowed her to go to Mass despite her poor condition. Her condition was incurable, he replied, but Sister was an extraordinary nun, so he did not take any notice of that. Others in her state would never rise, but he had seen her holding on to the wall as she walked to the chapel.

Sister Faustina's health was deteriorating all the time and the end of her life on earth was approaching. Aware of this, she took her leave of the community. In August 1938 she wrote a letter to Mother General Michaela Moraczewska: "Dearest Reverend Mother, I feel this is our last conversation on earth. I feel very, very weak and am writing with a trembling hand. I am suffering as much as I can bear. Jesus does not ask you to suffer beyond your capacity. The grace of God is as great as the suffering. I put all my trust in God and His holy will. I am filled with an ever greater longing for God. I do not fear death, my soul abounds in great peace." She expressed her thanks for all the good she had received from Mother General and the Congregation, she begged forgiveness for her transgressions against the rule, she asked for their sisterly love, prayer and a blessing in the hour of death. She concluded the letter with the words, "Farewell, Dearest Mother, we shall see each other at the feet of God's throne. And now praised be the Divine Mercy in us and through us."

It was at Prądnik Hospital that she spoke for the last time with her Vilnian spiritual director, Father Sopoćko, who was in Kraków in early September 1938 for the Congress of Theological Institutions and had the opportunity to visit his extraordinary penitent before she died and hear instructions directly from her relating to the work of Mercy which Jesus had initiated through her services. Sister Faustina told him that his chief concern was to be the establishment of the Feast of the Divine Mercy in the Church and not to worry too much about the new congregation, and that there would be signs which would let him know what to do in this matter. She said that she would soon die and that she had finished all she had had to write and pass on. During their last Prądnik meeting her Vilnian spiritual director was a witness to an ecstasy. After having said good-bye to Sister Faustina he left her room, but on his way out remembered that he had not left her the booklets with the prayers to the Divine Mercy Jesus had given her. When he returned and opened the door to her room he found her levitating over the bed and absorbed in prayer. "Her eyes were fixed on an invisible object, and her pupils slightly dilated, for some time she did not take any notice of me, and I did not want to disturb her and was intending to leave, but soon she came round, noticed me and apologised for not hearing me knock or enter. I gave her the prayers and said good-bye, and she said, 'See you in heaven.' The last time I visited her, on 26 September in the Łagiewniki Convent, she did not want to talk to me, or perhaps she couldn't any longer, saying she was in communion with the Heavenly Father. Indeed she gave the impression of a supernatural being. I no longer had any doubts that what she wrote in her diary about Holy Communion being administered to her in hospital by an angel was absolutely true."

On her return from hospital (17 September 1938) Sister Faustina waited in the convent's infirmary for the moment of her passage from this world to the Father's House. The Sisters took turns in keeping a vigil by her bedside. The superior of the house, Mother Irena Krzyżanowska, liked to visit her there, and observed Sister Faustina's great calm and a strange charm about her. The tension regarding the accomplishing of the work of Mercy entrusted her by the Lord had gone. "There will be a Feast of Divine Mercy, I see it, all I want is to do God's will," she told Mother Superior. Asked by her if she was pleased to be dying in our Congregation she replied, "Yes. You'll see that the Congregation will be solaced by me." Shortly before she died she sat up in bed and asked Mother Superior to come up closer. Then she whispered, "Jesus wants to elevate me and make me a saint." "I observed a profound gravity in her, and had a strange feeling that Sister Faustina took this assurance as a gift from the Divine Mercy, without a trace of pride," Mother Irena recalled.

During her last meeting with Father Sopoćko Sister Faustina said she would die in ten days' time. And that is exactly what happened. On the afternoon of 5 October 1938 Father Andrasz arrived at the Łagiewniki Convent and for the last time granted Sister Faustina absolution and administered the Sacrament of the Sick. That day at supper time a bell was heard. The sisters in the refectory got up from table and went upstairs, where Sister Faustina was lying in her room. By her bedside were the chaplain Father Teodor Czaputa, and Mother Superior Irena Krzyżanowska, while the rest of the Sisters stood in the corridor. Together they said the prayers for the dying, after which Sister Faustina told Mother Superior that she would not die yet. The sisters went down to the evening service. Sister Eufemia Traczyńska, a young nun in her juniorate, had heard from Sister Amelia Socha that Sister Faustina was bound to become a saint. Sister Eufemia wanted to see how saints die, but she could not exactly count on her superior granting her permission to attend a sister dying of tuberculosis. She prayed to the souls in purgatory to wake her when the time came for Sister Faustina to die. "I went to bed at the usual time," Sister Eufemia recollected, "and was soon asleep. Suddenly someone woke me up. 'Sister, if you want to be by Sister Faustina when she dies, get up now.' I knew at once it was an error. The sister who had come to wake up Sister Amelia had gone to the wrong cell and woken me instead. I woke Sister Amelia, put on my overall and bonnet and dashed to the infirmary. Sister Amelia arrived after me. It was around eleven at night. When we got there Sister Faustina as if opened her eyes and gave a faint smile, and then bowed her head and …Sister Amelia said that probably she had just died.

I looked at Sister Amelia but said nothing. We continued to pray. The Candlemas candle continued to burn."

The funeral took place on 7 October, the Feast of Our Lady of the Rosary. Not only the sisters but also their charges and even the farm hands came down to pray in the crypt where Sister Faustina's coffin stood. One of them was Janek, who was said to be lapsed. He stood by Sister Faustina's coffin and cried, so great was the impression she had made on him that apparently after the funeral he was converted. There was also Jadzia, a blind charge, who told of her unusual experiences. After the funeral service, which was conducted by Father Władysław Wojtoń SJ attended by two other priests, the sisters themselves carried Sister Faustina's coffin down to the community's cemetery in the garden.

Sister Faustina had achieved the fullness of union with God and sang a hymn of joy in honour of His unfathomable Mercy. For us on earth she left a promise: "Poor earth, I will not forget you. Although I feel that I will be immediately immersed in God as in an ocean of happiness, that will not be an obstacle to my returning to earth to encourage souls and incite them to trust in God's mercy. Indeed, this immersion in God will give me the possibility of boundless action."

12.

"My mission will not end at my death"

Sister Faustina's prophetic mission was kept strictly secret during her lifetime. No-one knew about it except for Father Michał Sopoćko, Father Józef Andrasz, and some of her superiors. After her death, when World War Two came, Sister Faustina's Vilnian confessor Father Sopoćko disclosed the name of the initiator of the devotion to Divine Mercy, which was spreading. His disclosure was followed by the same in the Congregation of the Sisters of Our Lady of Mercy. Mother General Michaela Moraczewska visited all the Congregation's houses and spoke on the great mission for which God had chosen Sister Faustina. "What most struck me about Sister Faustina," she wrote after her death, "and still strikes me today as an extraordinary phenomenon, especially in the last months of her illness, was her absolute self-oblivion for the sake of the dissemination of the worship of Divine Mercy. She never showed the slightest doubts as to the authenticity of her mission nor fear of death, she was absolutely engrossed in the leading light of her entire life – the devotion to Divine Mercy.

During the terrible war years the devotion to the Divine Mercy spread rapidly, bringing a ray of light and hope into the darkness. As the devotion became more and more widely known the opinion of Sister Faustina's sainthood grew as well. Pilgrims started to come to her grave in the Łagiewniki Convent and pray for her intercession. In the convent chapel Father Andrasz blessed another picture of the Merciful Jesus painted in accordance with Sister Faustina's instructions and started special services in honour of the Divine Mercy. They were attended by crowds from the City of Kraków and its environs. One of the people who came to worship before this image was Karol Wojtyła, a young labourer from the Solvay quarry which neighboured on the convent, who had already become familiar with the devotion to Divine Mercy in the forms of worship prescribed by Sister Faustina. After his ordination on the third Sunday of each month he celebrated Divine Mercy services in this chapel and, as the community records say, preached wonderful sermons on this mystery of faith.

In 1965, after he was consecrated Bishop of Kraków, he initiated a diocesan process for the beatification and canonisation of Sister Faustina. This required a great deal of courage, as ever since 1959 there had been a notification by the Holy See in force prohibiting the spread of the devotion to Divine Mercy in the forms prescribed by Sister Faustina. The notification had been issued owing to an erroneous translation of her diary and resulting inappropriate forms of worship. Under Communism maintaining contact between Poland and the Holy See was not at all easy, and so it was difficult to refute the Holy See's objections to the writings of Sister Faustina and the forms of worship. This period, which Sister Faustina had foretold, contributed to the theological analysis of her writings and the making of the right foundations for the practice of the devotion. Clear on the point that this situation was no obstacle to the initiating of a beatification process, Cardinal Karol Wojtyła lost no time and completed the diocesan stage, sending the documentation up to the Rome, where the Congregation for the Causes of Saints continued to examine the heroic virtues of Sister Faustina, and later the miracle wrought at Sister Faustina's grave for Mrs. Maureen Digan from the USA.

On Divine Mercy Sunday, 18 April 1993, the Holy Father John Paul II raised Sister Faustina to the glory of the altars. During his homily in St. Peter's Square, Rome, he referred to her words, "I know very well that my mission will not end at my death, that's when it will start." And he observed, "That's exactly what happened. Sister Faustina's mission continues and is bringing wondrous fruit. How marvellously her Divine Mercy service is making its way around the world and winning so many human hearts! It is undoubtedly a sign of our times – a sign of our 20th century. Alongside its achievements which have by far eclipsed those of previous ages, the balance of the century now drawing to a close also carried deep anxiety for the future. Where, if not in Divine Mercy, will the world find rescue and the light of hope? People of faith feel this perfectly well!"

After the revocation of the Holy See's notification in 1978, John Paul II's encyclical *Dives in Misericordia* and Sister Faustina's beatification, the devotion to Divine Mercy spread throughout the world in a dramatic manner. In the Diocese of Kraków the Feast of Divine Mercy was being celebrated on the first Sunday after Easter already from 1985, and throughout Poland on the grounds of a papal decree from 1995. By that time over a million pilgrims from all over the world were coming annually to the miraculous picture of the Merciful Jesus and the relics of Sister Faustina laid to rest in the altar of the chapel in Łagiewniki Convent, Kraków. After the Holy See's examination of the next miracle, the healing of Father Ronald Pytel of Baltimore of an incurable heart disease, the Holy Father John Paul II numbered Sister Faustina among the saints of the Catholic Church.

The canonisation ceremony was held on the Feast of Divine Mercy, 30 April 2000, in St. Peter's Square, Rome, and was attended by bishops and priests, nuns, and huge crowds of pilgrims from all over the world. Thanks to a satellite television link religious and lay pilgrims gathered in the Łagiewniki Shrine of Divine Mercy in Kraków could participate in the ceremony. Several decades earlier the event had been described by Sister Faustina: "at once I saw myself in Rome, in the Holy Father's chapel and at the same time I was in our chapel. And the celebration of the Holy Father and the entire Church was closely connected with our chapel and, in a very special way, with our Congregation. And I took part in the solemn celebration simultaneously here and in Rome, for the celebration was so closely connected with Rome that, even as I write, I cannot distinguish the two but I am writing it down as I saw it. I saw the Lord Jesus in our chapel, exposed in the monstrance on the high altar. The chapel was adorned as for a feast, and on that day anyone who wanted to come was allowed in. The crowd was so enormous that the eye could not take it all in. Everyone was participating in the celebrations with great joy, and many of them obtained what they desired. The same celebration was held in Rome, and the Holy Father, with all the clergy, was celebrating this Feast, and then suddenly I saw Saint Peter, who stood between the altar and the Holy Father. I could not hear what Saint Peter said but I saw that the Holy Father understood his words..."

During that ceremony, held in the Jubilee Year, the Holy Father instituted the Feast of Divine Mercy for the entire Church and passed on to the world the prophetic mission of Mercy for the third millennium of faith. "I pass it on to all people," he said, "so that they will learn to know ever better the true face of God and the true face of their brethren." Two years later he made his second pilgrimage as Pope to the Łagiewniki Shrine, and in the basilica church he had just consecrated entrusted the whole world to the Divine Mercy. He said that he wanted the message of God's merciful love preached here thanks to the mediation of Sister Faustina to reach all the earth's inhabitants and fill their hearts with hope. He wanted that message to radiate out from Łagiewniki to the whole of Poland and the entire world, and Jesus' promise to be fulfilled that "a spark which would prepare the world for Jesus' final coming" would issue from this place (cf. the Diary, 1732). He asked people to kindle that spark of God's grace and to transmit the fire of mercy to the world. For it was in Divine Mercy that the world would find peace, and mankind happiness.

Today there is probably no country left without an image of the Merciful Jesus. The Feast of the Divine Mercy has entered the universal Church's liturgical calendar for good. The Chaplet to the Divine Mercy is recited even in obscure languages, and the prayer at the hour of Jesus' death on the cross, the Hour of Mercy, is becoming more and more popular. The Apostolic Movement of Divine Mercy, the "congregation" based on Sister Faustina's mystical experience and charism which Jesus asked her to found, today comprises a variety of congregations, associations, confraternities, apostolates and individuals joining in the accomplishment of her mission. They are bringing the message of Mercy into the world through the witness of their lives, works, words, and prayer. The Congregation of the Sisters of Our Lady of Mercy has fully adopted Sister Faustina's prophetic mission, and on 25 August 1995 recognised her as its Spiritual Foundress. Theologians inspired by Sister Faustina are examining the mystery of Divine Mercy; apostles of Divine Mercy from her school are training in the attitude of trust in God and mercy for their neighbour, love of the Eucharist and the Church, and learning the true veneration of Our Lady of Mercy. Many churches dedicated to the Divine Mercy, the Merciful Jesus, or St. Faustina are being founded in Poland and throughout the world. Numerous new Divine Mercy shrines have sprung up to preach the truth of God's merciful love for each human being. The image of God who is not only just but also merciful and wants us to follow His example with regard to our neighbours is becoming established in Christian lives. Sister Faustina's mission certainly did not end at her death. It is continuing and bringing forth wondrous fruit. Perhaps, on account of what she has brought into the life and teaching of the Church, one day she will be ranked among the doctors of the Church?

The Beatification
and Canonisation Miracles

The Łagiewniki archives of the Congregation of the Sisters of Our Lady of Mercy contain thousands of thank-you letters for diverse graces. They include spectacular cures from a variety of diseases, and even greater graces associated with spiritual healing, many of them spiritual restorations to godly life. There are testimonials of God's intervention in everyday problems at work, in school or at home; letters of gratitude for the grace of a long-awaited child, peace and harmony in the family or neighbourhood... A few have been published in the quarterly magazine *Orędzie Miłosierdzia*. They reveal an extraordinary world, the world of God's mercy, open to those who trust in God and use this instrument to seek graces for themselves and for others. These testimonials bring tangible evidence that Jesus is fulfilling His promises entered in St. Faustina's *Diary*.

"Souls that trust boundlessly are a great comfort to Me," He said, "because I pour all the treasures of My graces into them. I rejoice that they ask for much, because it is My desire to give much, very much. On the other hand, I am sad when souls ask for little, when they narrow their hearts."

In this publication we shall cite only those miracles which the Holy See examined and recognised for Sister Faustina's beatification and canonisation process.

I didn't believe in miracles
Testimony of Maureen Digan

I'm sure that after my testimony some, if not all of you will ask, "Why her and not me or one of my dear ones?" Well, I keep asking myself the same question: why me and not my son, who has been ill for years?

At the age of 15 I was struck down with a disease called lymphedema. Between the age of 15 and 20 I had 50 operations. For a decade I was in and out of hospital all the time. I was hospitalised for periods from 1 week to 12 months at a time. At 19 I had a spinal operation and for 2 years was paralysed from the hips down. When I was 20 I had my first amputation. But the disease became so aggravated in the rest of my leg that I had to have it amputated up to the hip.

My husband Bob, a deeply religious person of tremendous faith and prayer, felt that he should take his family, that is myself and our sick son, to Poland. He went to Eden Hill, Stockbridge, the national shrine of the Divine Mercy in the USA, and talked the matter over with Father Seraphim Michalenko, asking if he could accompany us on our trip to Poland. Father Serafin, who was handling the cause of Sister Faustina in the USA, received consent from his superiors and we set off on the difficult journey to Kraków.

On 28 March 1981 I went to confession in Kraków. It must have been my first confession for many, many years. I felt much closer to Jesus and Sister Faustina, but maybe not close enough. That evening, 28 March, we prayed at the tomb of Sister Faustina, especially for a cure. Still somewhat mistrustful, I said to Sister Faustina, "Okay, Faustina I came a long way, now do something." And the pain stopped, the swelling disappeared. I thought it must have been a symptom of neurosis as I didn't believe in miracles. I stuffed my shoe with a napkin so that no-one should notice my swelling was gone.

And I stopped taking my medicine. From that moment on my disease disappeared completely. I had visited four different doctors, who told me that my disease was incurable, that it never went into remission, and did not respond to any medication.

Our Lord chooses whoever He wants. We thank him from the bottom of our hearts for my healing, which will help to beatify Sister Faustina. It's absolutely true what you read in her Diary: "The greater the misery, the greater the right to My mercy."

After the article published
in *Orędzie Miłosierdzia* 13 (1992),
the tape-recorded testimony,
and the Divine Mercy website
<http://www.thedivinemercy.org/message/stfaustina/graces.php>

Ron, someone has intervened for you

The Testimony of Father Ronald Pytel

On 16 November 1999, the doctors invited by the Congregation for the Causes of Saints to examine my case voted on the matter and declared that there was no medical explanation for the immediate cure of the seriously damaged left ventricle of my heart. On 9 December a Vatican theological committee confirmed this was a miracle attributed to the intercession of Blessed Sister Faustina Kowalska. This was followed by a session of the cardinals' committee, and on 20 December the decree on the miracle was promulgated in the presence of the Holy Father Pope John Paul II.

My name is Ronald Pytel and I am an American of Polish extraction. My grandparents came from Poland. I am parish priest of Holy Rosary Parish, Baltimore, Maryland (USA). Our parish is the diocesan shrine of the Divine Mercy. As a young boy, I remember seeing the image of Divine Mercy in our school with the inscription, "Jezu, ufam Tobie!" (Jesus, I trust in you!). I was ordained a priest 26 years ago and after some time joined in the work to disseminate the devotion to Divine Mercy. Since the year of Sister Faustina's beatification there is a Divine Mercy service in English in our church every second Sunday of the month, and a Polish Divine Mercy service every third Sunday of the month. Also every Thursday we have a continuous novena to the Divine Mercy. Our parish is promoting the devotion to Divine Mercy by organising retreats, lectures, and pilgrimages. So when I became ill, my own and my parishioners' prayers were addressed to the Divine Mercy through the intercession of Blessed Faustina.

I fell ill in 1995. All through the winter and spring I did not feel well. The symptoms were indicative of a cold and an allergy, and later bronchitis. I was out of breath from mounting the stairs up to the first floor and I was coughing all the time. I went to see a doctor, who confirmed the diagnosis: allergic bronchitis. He also observed that the heart murmur I had had since childhood had intensified and he sent me for a Doppler echocardiogram. The test showed that my aorta valve was constricted due to a calcium deposit, and pumping only 20 percent of my normal blood-flow. In essence, I was in cardiac heart failure.

On 8 June 1995 I had an appointment with Dr. Nicholas Fortuin, a well-known cardiologist of Johns Hopkins University Hospital in Baltimore. He studied my echocardiogram and confirmed the diagnosis, constriction of the aortic valve. He prescribed medicine for me and sent me home, ordering me to stay in bed until my operation at Johns Hopkins University Hospital, which was due on 14 June 1995. On the way to the hospital my best friend, Father Larry Gesy, said, "Don't worry, Ron, this is all about Divine Mercy." Although I was not pleased at the thought of the forthcoming operation, I just knew all would be fine. I read Sister Faustina's diary, a copy of which I had packed to take to the hospital, and said the Divine Mercy Chaplet every day.

After the operation Dr. Peter Green, the surgeon, spoke to Father Gesy and told him that my heart was seriously damaged due to the constricted aortic valve which did not allow normal blood-flow. I would have been in danger of dying if I had not had the operation. After another examination Dr. Fortuin told him that he could not predict exactly how my heart would behave, but it was certain I would never be able to resume a normal life. He looked really concerned as he told him that nobody could give me a guarantee that I would live, and that my prospects of a long life were small. His diagnosis was not at all optimistic. My left ventricle had suffered serious damage. My friend gradually disclosed this diagnosis to me.

On 5 October, 1995, the feast of then-Blessed Faustina Kowalska, the parish celebrated an all-day vigil before the Blessed Sacrament. We recited the Divine Mercy Chaplet, the rosary, and other prayers. The day finished with Holy Mass in preparation for the Holy Father's visit to Baltimore on 8 October 1995. I was chief celebrant at the Mass and preached a sermon on trusting in God and how God had exercised His mercy on me. Later that evening, a group of individuals prayed for my return to health, while I venerated a first-class relic of Blessed Faustina. During the prayer, I rested in the Holy Spirit. I lay on the floor for about 15 minutes. I was totally conscious and awake, but I could not move. I felt as if I were paralysed, as the healing ministry and my parishioners gathered around me and prayed.

Later that evening I realised I had forgotten to take my medicine. I took it around midnight and prepared for bed. Then I started to feel a pain in my heart every time I took a deep breath. I had never had such a pain before, only the pain of the operation wound. It was something new for me, something I had never experienced. I thought that I must have been over-active during the day. After a while I realised that the pain had increased when I took my medicine. Next day I did not take my medicine at all and there was no pain.

I phoned Dr. Fortuin to tell him about the problem. I felt that my heart medication was causing the pain. Dr. Fortuin told me it was the best drug for my heart disease and that my body had tolerated it for two months with no side-effects. He said that if my body was reacting in this way, to take half the dose one day and the full dose every other day and phone him after a week. I felt better when I was taking half the dose. The pain was less intense and passed sooner. I phoned Dr. Fortuin and informed him about what I had observed. He told me to continue taking half the dose until my next visit, in 9 days' time.

On 9 November I saw Dr. Fortuin. After the initial examination I had a Doppler echocardiogram. The doctor looked at the results of the test and asked me into his office. He stared at me in silence for what seemed like an eternity and then he spoke, "Ron, someone has intervened for you." "What does that mean?" I asked. He said, "Your heart is normal." "What?" I was surprised. "Your heart is normal," he repeated. Dr. Green suggested repeating the echocardiogram to see if the left ventricle had improved. "No, no… we're talking about a completely normal heart," said Dr. Fortuin. "My prognosis for your state of health was not very optimistic. I can't explain it. You don't need any restrictions or any medicine at all," he continued. ""I'll see you again after a year's time for a checkup." "A year?" I asked, surprised. "Yes, a year. Your heart is completely healthy." When I left his office I phoned Father Gesy and told him what I'd heard from Dr. Fortuin. "We have the miracle we've been praying for," he said.

In November 1996 an official tribunal committee was appointed in the Archdiocese of Baltimore to examine the opinions the doctors had made under oath and the testimony of witnesses concerning my state of health. When the diocesan process had been completed Father Seraphim Michalenko, Vice-Postulator for the cause of Sister Faustina in the United States, took the sealed documents from the Baltimore tribunal and in December 1996 we took them to Rome. The documentation comprised over 800 pages of medical data and about 500 pages of statements made under oath.

I know that Sister Faustina interceded for me with Jesus and that His love touched and healed me. It's as simple as that.

Translated from the text published
in *Orędzie Miłosierdzia* 34 (2000), p. 6–7,
with extracts from the article "Trail of mercy:
the legacy of Father Ron Pytel," by Susan Brinkmann,
published in *The Catholic Standard and Times*
<http://www.cst-phl.com/050317/prayer.html>

Biographical Calendar

of the life and mission
of St. Faustina

25 August 1905	Helena Kowalska born in the village of Głogowiec (Poland).
27 August 1905	Baptised in the Parish of St. Casimir, Świnice Warckie.
1914	First Holy Communion.
1917	Starts school.
1921	Goes into domestic service in the household of Kazimierz Bryszewski and his wife Leokadia in Aleksandrów Łódzki.
1922	Stays at the house of her uncle Michał Rapacki in Łódź and works as a maid for some Tertiary Franciscan ladies.
2 February 1923	Goes into domestic service in the household of Marcjanna Sadow-

	ska, owner of a shop on the Abramowskiego, Łódź.
July 1924	Leaves for Warsaw to enter a convent. Works for Aldona Lipszycowa at Ostrówek in the District of Klembów. First visit in the convent of the Congregation of the Sisters of Our Lady of Mercy. Provisionally received by Mother Michaela Moraczewska.
1 August 1925	Enters the convent of the Congregation of the Sisters of Our Lady of Mercy, ulica Żytnia, Warsaw.
August 1925	Stays at Skolimów for a course of health improvement.
1925	Postulancy under the direction of Mother Janina Bartkiewicz in the Congregation's house in Warsaw
23 January 1926	Arrives in Kraków to complete her postulancy and two-year novitiate under the direction of Mother Małgorzata Gimbutt and Mother Maria Józefa Brzoza.
30 April 1926	Takes the veil, and receives the name Sister Maria Faustyna in religion.
30 April 1928	Makes her first religious vows of chastity, poverty, and obedience.
31 October 1928	Leaves for the Warsaw house to work in the kitchen.

21 February 1929	Leaves for Wilno (now Vilnius, Lithuania) to replace a sister going on her 3rd probation.
June 1929	Leaves for the Congregation's new house on the Hetmańska in the Grochów district of Warsaw.
7 July 1929	Leaves for Kiekrz, to work in the kitchen as a replacement for a sister who is sick.
October 1929	Stays in the motherhouse on the Żytnia in Warsaw.
May – June 1930	Arrives in Płock and works in the bakery shop. Stays in the Płock daughter-house at Biała (10 km from Płock).
22 February 1931	Beginning of her prophetic mission. Has first vision of the Merciful Jesus and is instructed to have a picture painted.
February 1931	Jesus instructs her to have the Feast of Divine Mercy celebrated on the first Sunday after Easter.
November 1932	Leaves for Warsaw for her 3rd probation.
November 1932	Retreat at Walendów. Father Edmund Elter SJ hears her confession and gives the first confirmation of the supernatural provenance of the visions.

1 December 1932	Starts 3rd probation under the direction of Mother Małgorzata Gimbutt.
1 May 1933	Makes her perpetual vows in Kraków.
27 May 1933	Leaves for Wilno. Works in the convent garden.
June 1933	First meeting with Father Michał Sopoćko, her confessor and spiritual director, whom God chose to assist her in the accomplishment of her prophetic mission.
2 January 1934	First visit to the studio of artist Eugeniusz Kazimirowski
26-28 April 1935	First public display of the picture of the Merciful Jesus, Ostra Brama, Wilno.
May 1935	The idea of a new congregation is born.
13-14 September 1935	Jesus teaches her the Chaplet to the Divine Mercy
21 March 1936	Leaves for Warsaw.
25 March 1936	Arrival at Walendów, followed by stay at Derdy.
12 May 1936	Arrives in Kraków.
9 December 1936	Leaves for Prądnik Hospital.
27 March 1937	Returns from hospital to the Łagiewniki (Kraków) convent.
29 July 1937	Leaves for treatment in the health resort Rabka.

10 August 1937	Returns from Rabka to Kraków.
October 1937	Jesus makes known the Hour of Mercy.
21 April 1938	Second stay in Prądnik Hospital.
17 September 1938	Returns from hospital to the Łagiewniki convent.
5 October 1938	Departs for the Lord's House.
7 October 1938	Funeral.
21 October 1965	By the decision of Cardinal Karol Wojtyła the diocesan process of the life and heroic virtues of Sister Faustina starts.
25 November 1966	Sister Faustina's body is transferred from the tomb in the cemetery to the chapel and laid to rest beneath the chapel floor.
20 September 1967	Cardinal Wojtyła completes the diocesan information process and sends the documentation to Rome.
18 April 1993	The Holy Father John Paul II beatifies Sister Faustina in St. Peter's Square, Rome. Sister Faustina's relics are deposited on the altar below the miraculous picture of the Merciful Jesus in the Shrine of the Divine Mercy at Łagiewniki, Kraków.
7 June 1997	Pilgrimage of the Holy Father John Paul II to the Shrine of the Divine Mercy at Łagiewniki, Kra-

	ków. The Holy Father prays before the holy picture of the Merciful Jesus and Sister Faustina's relics.
20 April 2000	The Holy Father John Paul II canonises Sister Faustina in St. Peter's Square, Rome. Satellite TV transmission of the ceremony in Rome and Łagiewniki. Foundation of the Feast of the Divine Mercy for the universal Church.
17 August 2002	Second pilgrimage of the Holy Father John Paul II to the Shrine of the Divine Mercy at Łagiewniki, Kraków. During the consecration ceremony for the new basilica the Holy Father entrusts the whole world to the Divine Mercy.